OFF THE BEATEN TRACK

Volume III: North Georgia

Jim Parham

WMC Publishing

Jim Parham's *OFF THE BEATEN TRACK Mountain Bike Guide Series:*

Volume I: A Guide to Mountain Biking in Western North Carolina—The Smokies

Volume II: A Guide to Mountain Biking in Western North Carolina—Pisgah

Volume IV: A Guide to Mountain Biking in East Tennessee

Volume V: A Guide to Mountain Biking in Northern Virginia

Volume VI: A Guide to Mountain Biking in West Virginia—Northern Highlands

Also by Jim Parham:
49 Fun & Inexpensive Things To Do In The Smokies With Children

WMC Publishing, P.O. Box 158, Almond, NC 28702

ISBN 0-9631861-9-1 $12.95
ISSN 1076-6189

Cover design by Ron Roman

A great deal of information is contained in this book, and every effort has been made to provide this information as accurately as possible. Roads and trails, however, can change with time; some roads and trails may not be marked by signs; distances may vary with individual cyclocomputers; and land agency rules and regulations are subject to interpretation and change. There are risks inherent in the sport of mountain biking. *The author and publisher accept no responsibility for inaccuracies or for damages incurred while attempting any of the routes listed.*

Printed in the United States on recycled paper.

ACKNOWLEDGMENTS

It is important to me and to others that the details of this revised edition be as accurate as possible. A number of people came forth to help insure this and I am very grateful for their help.

Jay Franklin, president of the Southern Off-Road Bicycle Association (SORBA), took the time to identify most of the newer routes in the north Georgia mountains and, believe me, he knows a lot—he personally helped build a quite a few of them.

This is also a good place to say a very special thanks to SORBA itself. If not for the hard work and dedication of the individuals that represent this organization, many of the trails in this book and the ones that you as a mountain biker in Georgia ride would not exist. Many days when they could otherwise be out riding their bikes, various members spend time building and maintaining trails, raising money to be used for trail upkeep, and fostering relationships with public land managers so that trails will remain open to cycling use. I encourage you to help support the work of SORBA by becoming a member yourself. You'll find a membership application in the back of this book. They do hard work, but they also have a lot of fun.

Thanks also to Peach Keller, Larry Thomas and Edwin Dale from the US Forest Service. Peach and Larry took the time to meet with me and fill me in with the latest updates for mountain bike use in the Chattahoochee National Forest. In addition, Peach and Edwin kept me updated of changes in new parking lot designations right up until press time. The Chattahoochee National Forest also deserves some special recognition. This forest is very proactive toward mountain bike use. There are quite a number of designated bike trails in the forest and numerous new trails are planned for the future.

Finally, Mike Palmeri, owner of Recycled Cycles in Ellijay, took the initiative to organize a meeting with SORBA and the US Forest Service at the very onset of the revision of this book. Many of these trails are just out Mike's back door, so if you find yourself near Ellijay, be sure to stop in at his shop for the latest trail information, any repairs, accessories, or just to say hello.

*A Guide to
Mountain Biking in
North Georgia*

Volume III

Jim Parham

TABLE OF CONTENTS

THE TRAILS

MOST DIFFICULT TRAILS ————————— 64

REGIONAL INFORMATION ———————— 78

INTRODUCTION

In the north Georgia mountains it's easy to see why mountain biking is the fastest growing recreational activity on our nation's public lands. Most any day, when the weather's right (which is most any time of year), people flock to the hills with their bikes. In fact, use has grown considerably since this book was first published. Since then, land managers and the Atlanta-based Southern Off-Road Bicycle Association (SORBA) have reacted in a way that could serve as a model for other states to follow. In the Chattahoochee National Forest, in several of Georgia's state parks, and in some of the Department of Natural Resources' wildlife management areas, new mountain bike trails have been built, routes have been reblazed and renamed, existing trails are consistently maintained, new trailheads have been established, and parking areas have been added. And what's just as exciting are the number of trails that haven't been built *yet*, but are flagged, marked, and will be constructed in the next few years. This new edition reflects those changes and additions as well as including all the best rides from the original version.

It's no wonder so many people love to ride in North Georgia—it's a great place for mountain biking. The mountains are chock full of trails and forest roads that can be linked together for some really fun rides. In the northwest corner of the state is Pigeon Mountain. Flat on top and almost hollow with caves, this spur off Lookout Mountain has a single track network of over 40 miles. To the east, across the great valley, are the Cohutta Mountains with their many remote and sometimes rugged trails. In and around the towns of Blue Ridge, Ellijay and Dahlonega you'll find the Aska Trail System, the popular Bull Mountain area, Amicalola Falls State Park, Cooper Creek and Carters Lake. Farther to the east is Helen, site of a big NORBA National race each year. On the eastern boundary is the newly formed Tallulah Gorge State Park, with a number of new bike trails in the works, as well.

Good riding is just part of the experience. The mountains themselves are over 230 million years old. Rounded off by time and covered with lush vegetation, from a distance they appear gentle and smooth. Once in their heart, however, you'll find them as rugged as they come—complete with waterfalls, cliffs and gorges. Peaks rise to over 4,000 feet, and on clear days you can see forever. You'll find single track trails that travel through remote valleys, along precipitous mountain ridges and through dense forests. Some are steep, rocky and tortuous; others are smooth, fast and relatively easy. Complementing the trails are forest roads that snake up the valleys and traverse the highest ridges. Some have gates to keep motor vehicles out, while others are so lightly traveled it's rare to see a car. They are good to ride in wet weather when the trails may be muddy. By linking these roads and trails together you can create routes that can be ridden in as little as an hour or as long as an entire day.

One of the best things about mountain biking in North Georgia is that it is a year-round activity. Although a few winter days can be quite cold, most are not too cold, and snow is rare. Summer days are hot, but once in the shade of the mountains, you'll find riding to be very pleasant. Of course, spring and fall temperatures are almost always perfect.

With the changes of the season, so change the type of users you are likely to see while out on the trail. In summer you'll encounter tourists of all kinds. Most come to escape the heat of the Deep South. They may be hiking, fishing, camping, tubing in the creek, or biking like yourself. In the fall, the number of cars with "leaf peepers" inside picks up on the forest roads. Give them a wide berth, as they tend to be looking up most of the time. Late fall and through the winter is hunting season, so be prepared to see folks with guns in the woods. Several of the rides in this book are on wildlife management areas, and, if a big game hunt is planned, you're better off riding somewhere else that day. Check with the Georgia DNR Wildlife Resources Division (770/918-6404) for area hunt dates. Otherwise, be sure to wear a bright color like blaze orange while in the woods. Of course, spring in the north Georgia mountains is beautiful and a great time to ride.

Whether you are a seasoned expert or a first-time mountain biker, you will find plenty of routes in this book to choose from. I've rated the routes at three different levels: Easiest, More Difficult and Most Difficult. Keep in mind these ratings are relative to this book and the topography of North Georgia. It's best not to overestimate your ability level and to pay close attention to the time estimates, highlights, total distance and elevation profiles to get the most enjoyment out of every ride.

I think you'll be drawn to these mountains again and again.

J.P.
April, 1996

How To Use This Book

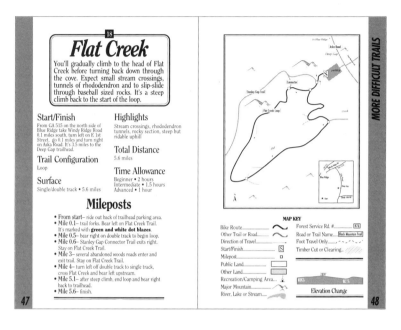

[18]

Flat Creek

You'll gradually climb to the head of Flat Creek before turning back down through the cove. Expect small stream crossings, tunnels of rhododendron and to slip-slide through baseball sized rocks. It's a steep climb back to the start of the loop.

Start/Finish
From GA 515 on the north side of Blue Ridge take Windy Ridge Road 0.1 miles south, turn left on E. 1st Street, go 0.1 miles and turn right on Aska Road. It's 3.5 miles to the Deep Gap trailhead.

Trail Configuration
Loop

Surface
Single/double track • 5.6 miles

Highlights
Stream crossings, rhododendron tunnels, rocky section, steep but ridable uphill

Total Distance
5.6 miles

Time Allowance
Beginner • 2 hours
Intermediate • 1.5 hours
Advanced • 1 hour

Mileposts
- **From start**– ride out back of trailhead parking area.
- **Mile 0.1**– trail forks. Bear left on Flat Creek Trail. It's marked with **green and white dot blazes**.
- **Mile 0.5**– bear right on double track to begin loop.
- **Mile 0.6**– Stanley Gap Connector Trail exits right. Stay on Flat Creek Trail.
- **Mile 3**– several abandoned woods roads enter and exit trail. Stay on Flat Creek Trail.
- **Mile 4**– turn left off double track to single track, cross Flat Creek and bear left upstream.
- **Mile 5.1**– after steep climb, end loop and bear right back to trailhead.
- **Mile 5.6**– finish.

MAP KEY

Bike Route		Forest Service Rd. #	[476]
Other Trail or Road		Road or Trail Name	[Black Mountain Trail]
Direction of Travel		Foot Travel Only	
Start/Finish	[S]	Timber Cut or Clearing	
Milepost	□		
Public Land			
Other Land			
Recreation/Camping Area	Ⓐ		
Major Mountain			
River, Lake or Stream			Elevation Change

47

48

Typical Route Description Pages

- The **route number** appears in either a circle, a square or a diamond at the top of the left-hand page. The number corresponds to the route number in the table of contents, and the circle (Easiest), square (More Difficult) or diamond (Most Difficult) indicates the route difficulty.

- **Route difficulty** (also shown vertically at the top right-hand corner of the right page) is relative to this book and the mountains of north Georgia. Many of these mountains are characterized by steep, rocky, rugged terrain. You can expect to find difficulties of every kind, including long uphills, steep downhills, boulder fields, stream crossings, and narrow, technical single track. Ratings are determined by technical difficulty, length, or a combination of the two.

- Below the **route name** is a brief description of the route's more noted highlights.

- **Start/Finish** indicates where the route begins and how to get there.

- **Trail Configuration** describes the type of route.

- **Surface** types include: single track, double track, forest road and pavement. This will show how many miles of each surface to expect.

- In the **Highlights** there will be a one or two-word description of things you can expect on the trail. For example: *ATV/ORV* means you may encounter all-terrain vehicles coming from either direction and you can expect the trail to show considerable wear and tear.

- **Total Distance** shows the number of miles you will travel.

- **Time Allowance** is a rough approximation of the time it will take you to ride the trail with *minimal* stops, according to your ability level.

- Each **milepost** corresponds to the adjoining map. The first milepost is at the Start/Finish and is represented by an Ⓢ on the map. There is a milepost for every turn or any other place of note, and each is represented by a □ on the map.

- The **maps** are oriented north, with roads or trails marked by name or number. All roads, trails, buildings, clearings and other features relevant to the route are shown, as well as the best direction of travel. Some of the routes listed in this book can be linked together for shorter or longer rides. When this is the case, those trails or roads are also shown on the map; however, no mileposts or directions are given for these. For particularly confusing-to-get-to routes, a map inset is included to aid in finding the start of the ride. **Maps are not drawn to scale**.

- The **Map Key** shows what each symbol represents, as well as indicating the shading used for different types of trails, roads or land. The main route is always shown in black.

- By looking at the **Elevation Change**, you can get a pretty good idea where the major hills are on the route, how high they will be, and the degree of steepness. It does not show every short rise or dip in the trail.

Other Sections

- There are two sections immediately following this page that cover **Rules of the Trail** and **Riding on North Georgia's Public Lands.** Knowing and following the rules and using good judgement are critical in keeping public land available to mountain bikers.

- On the **Orientation Pages** you'll find a map showing the location of the riding region relative to the rest of Georgia as well as an area map generally indicating where the start/finish is for each route.

- The **Regional Information** section has several subsections that will give you information on where to find and how to contact nearby bike shops, how to find places to stay in the area, a weather chart, and a membership form for the Southern Off-Road Bicycle Association.

Rules of the Trail

It takes only a few incidents of irresponsible or abusive trail riding to close a trail, a recreation area or an entire national forest to mountain bikers. Do your part to maintain trail access by observing the following rules of the trail formulated by the **International Mountain Bicycling Association (IMBA)**. IMBA's mission is to promote environmentally sound and socially responsible biking.

- **Ride on open trails only.** Respect trail and road closures, and avoid possible trespass on private land. Federal and state wilderness areas are closed to cycling. The way you ride will influence trail management decisions and policies.

- **Leave no trace.** Be sensitive to the dirt beneath you. Many trails in this part of Georgia can become quite muddy after periods of prolonged rain or freeze-thaw conditions. Consider riding on the hard packed forest roads at these times.

- **Control your bicycle.** Inattention for even a second can cause problems. Don't create danger for yourself and other trail users.

- **Always yield trail.** Make known your approach well in advance. A friendly greeting is considerate and works well; don't startle others. Show your respect when passing by slowing to a walking pace or even stopping. Anticipate meeting other trail users around corners and in blind spots.

- **Never spook animals.** When passing horses, use special care and follow directions from the horseback riders (ask if uncertain). Always ride slow and quietly through areas where wildlife may be feeding or nesting.

- **Plan ahead.** Know your equipment, your ability and the area in which you are riding—and prepare accordingly. Always wear a helmet.

For more information or to join the association contact:

IMBA
P.O. Box 7578
Boulder, CO 80306
303/545-9011

Riding on North Georgia's Public Lands

Chattahoochee National Forest

Most of the routes in this book are located within the Chattahoochee National Forest, which welcomes mountain bicycling use. You'll find the trails, trailheads and roads well marked and in good condition. There is no *specific* policy, but the general trails policy under which mountain bike use falls states: "Driving, riding, possessing, parking or leaving any kind of transportation on a developed trail not designated, and so posted, for that specific use" is prohibited. Therefore, any unsigned, developed trail should be considered closed to bicycles. Bikes are allowed on gated and closed Forest Service roads, unless signed otherwise. For more information, call 706/536-0541.

Crockford-Pigeon Mountain Wildlife Management Area

Pigeon Mountain is managed by the Georgia Department of Natural Resources and is regulated first and foremost for game management. It also contains over 40 miles of multiple-use trails that are great for mountain biking. At present, the entire mountain is open to bikes except for the Rocktown area. Riding is permitted anytime but I strongly suggest avoiding use during big game hunts, which usually occur in the late fall or early winter. For annual hunt dates and additional information, call 706/295-6041.

Georgia State Parks

At present in the north Georgia mountains, Unicoi State Park and Amicalola Falls State Park (a short section before entering the national forest) have mountain bike trails. Tallulah Gorge State Park has a number of trails planned to be completed sometime in 1996. The basic rule: Stay on the designated bike trails. You can look for more trails at other state parks in the future.

For more information, call:

Unicoi State Park   706/878-2824
Amicalola Falls State Park   706/265-8888
Tallulah Gorge State Park   706/754-8257

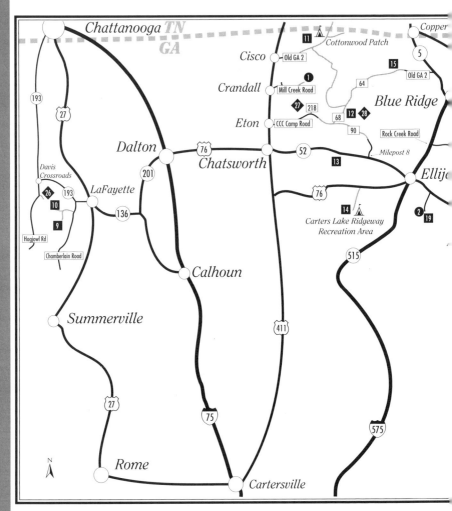

Chattanooga **TN**
GA

Copper

193

27

Cisco — ⬡ — Old GA 2

11 ⛺ Cottonwood Patch

5

15

Old GA 2

Crandall — 1 ⬡ Mill Creek Road

64

27 218

Blue Ridge

Eton — ⬡ CCC Camp Road

68 12 28

90

Dalton — 76

Davis Crossroads

201

52

13

Rock Creek Road

Milepost 8

Ellij

Chatsworth

LaFayette

26 193

10

9

136

76

14 ⛺

Ellij

2 19

Hogjowl Rd

Chamberlain Road

Carters Lake Ridgeway
Recreation Area

515

Calhoun

Summerville

411

N

27

75

575

Rome

Cartersville

Map Detail

Orientation Map

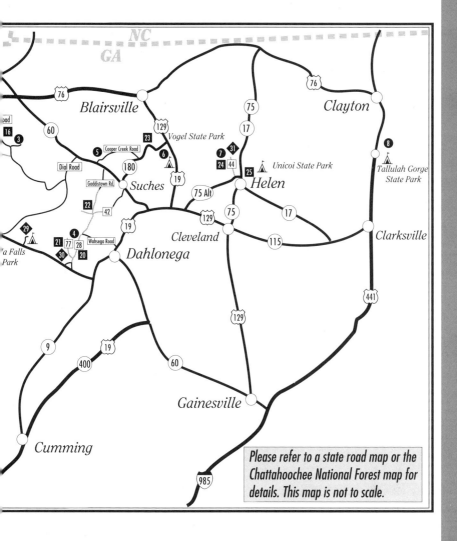

Please refer to a state road map or the Chattahoochee National Forest map for details. This map is not to scale.

● Easiest Trails

1 Rocky Flats
2 Red & White Loop
3 Long Branch
4 Wahsega
5 Cooper Creek
6 Sosebee Cove
7 Jasus Creek
8 Tallulah Gorge

■ More Difficult Trails

9 Pigeon Mountain
10 High Point
11 Iron Mountain
12 Bear Creek
13 Tatum Lead
14 Carters Lake
15 South Fork
16 Green Mountain
17 Stanley Gap
18 Flat Creek
19 River Loop
20 Turner Creek
21 Winding Stairs

22 Canada Creek
23 Duncan Ridge
24 Upper Hooch
25 Helen

◆ Most Difficult Trails

26 North Pocket
27 Windy Gap
28 Mountaintown Creek
29 Amicalola Falls
30 Bull Mountain
31 Tennessee Divide

EASIEST TRAILS

Rocky Flats

①

An easy ride with relatively few hills and lots of views of the surrounding mountains. Be ready for one really fast downhill with numerous large whoop-te-doos near the end of the loop.

Start/Finish

From Crandall, GA, go east 4 miles on Mill Creek Road (FS 630), to second Rocky Flats ORV sign.

Trail Configuration

Loop

Surface

Double track • 4.7 miles
Forest road • 1.1 miles

Highlights

ORV and ATV use, wildlife openings, timber cuts, whoop-te-doos, stream crossing

Total Distance

5.8 miles

Time Allowance

Beginner • 1 hour
Intermediate • 45 minutes
Advanced • 35 minutes

Mileposts

- **From start**– ride out ORV trail away from Mill Creek Road.
- **Mile 2.7**– road forks. Bear right on main road.
- **Mile 4.7**– steep downhill to stream crossing. Bear left up the hill after crossing the stream and then turn right onto Mill Creek Road.
- **Mile 5.8**– finish.

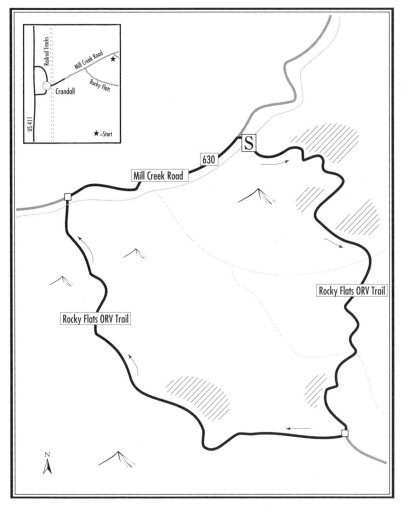

MAP KEY

Bike Route........................... ~

Other Trail or Road........... ~

Direction of Travel............... ⟶

Start/Finish............................ Ⓢ

Milepost................................... □

Public Land.......................

Other Land.......................

Recreation/Camping Area... ⛺

Major Mountain...................

River, Lake or Stream.....

Forest Service Rd. #.................. 476

Road or Trail Name..... Black Mountain Trail

Foot Travel Only....... ‐ ‐ ‐ ‐ ‐

Timber Cut or Clearing.. ////

1120'   1560'   960'

Elevation Change

Red & White Loop

This short little loop is a great place for beginners to test their skills. You'll find short sections of tight single track, but mostly the going is pretty easy. This route can easily be added to the more difficult River Loop for an all-out ride. It gets its name from the alternating red and white blazes on the trees.

Start/Finish

From GA 515 in Ellijay, take GA 52 east for 3.2 miles and turn right onto County Road 225. Go 0.4 miles and turn right into the Rich Mountain WMA Cartecay Track. Go 0.3 miles to start at the gate.

Trail Configuration

Loop

Surface

Single track • 2.2 miles
Gravel road • 0.4 miles

Highlights

Hidden turns, short technical stretch, grassy roadbed, wildlife openings

Total Distance

2.6 miles

Time Allowance

Beginner • 45 minutes
Intermediate • 30 minutes
Advanced • 20 minutes

Mileposts

- **From start**– ride past gate out gravel road.
- **Mile 0.1**– end of loop enters from right. Bear left.
- **Mile 0.2**– small clearing just past gate on right. Turn right over the dirt barricade onto **red & white blazed** trail.
- **Mile 0.4**– trail splits. Turn right. Look for blazes.
- **Mile 1.2**– wildlife opening. Stay to right side.
- **Mile 1.4**– wildlife opening. Stay to right side and then continue to the right on the grassy roadbed.
- **Mile 2.4**– gate, turn left.
- **Mile 2.6**– finish.

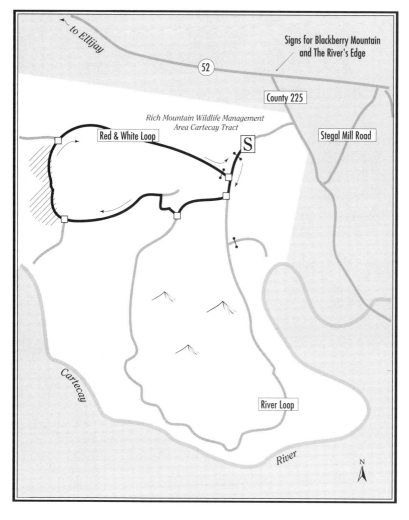

to Ellijay

Signs for Blackberry Mountain
and The River's Edge

52

County 225

Rich Mountain Wildlife Management
Area Cartecay Tract

Red & White Loop

S

Stegal Mill Road

Cartecay

River Loop

River

N

MAP KEY

Bike Route..........................	〰	Forest Service Rd. #.................	476
Other Trail or Road...........	〜	Road or Trail Name.....	Black Mountain Trail
Direction of Travel................	→	Foot Travel Only.......	- - ⌐ - ⌐ - ⌐
Start/Finish..............................	S	Timber Cut or Clearing..	/////
Milepost....................................	□		
Public Land......................	▭		
Other Land......................	▭		
Recreation/Camping Area...	⛺		
Major Mountain..................	⛰		
River, Lake or Stream.....	〰		

1600'

1400'

Elevation Change

③
Long Branch

The first half of this loop follows an old skid road through a timber cut (read: hot and exposed on a sunny summer day, muddy when wet). After crossing the creek, you'll tunnel through the shady rhododendron and hop over a few waterbars before a short hill climb back to the beginning of the loop.

Start/Finish

From GA 515 in Blue Ridge turn south onto Windy Ridge Road. Go 0.1 miles, turn left on E. 1st Street, go 0.1 miles and turn right on Aska Road. Continue another 5.9 miles and turn left onto Shady Falls Road. Go 0.2 miles to the Forest Service parking area on the left.

Trail Configuration

Loop with extension

Surface

Single/double track • 2.2 miles

Highlights

Views, stream crossing, waterbars, briar and mud potential, connects to Green Mountain Trail

Total Distance

2.2 miles

Time Allowance

Beginner • 45 minutes
Intermediate • 30 minutes
Advanced • 20 minutes

Mileposts

- **From start**– ride out of back of trailhead parking.
- **Mile 0.2**– fork. Start loop by taking trail to the left. The trail is marked with sporadic **white and green dot blazes**.
- **Mile 1.3**– Green Mountain Trail Connector enters from the left (marked by a **green dot**).
- **Mile 1.8**– bear right at trail fork.
- **Mile 2**– end loop. Continue back to trailhead.
- **Mile 2.2**– finish.

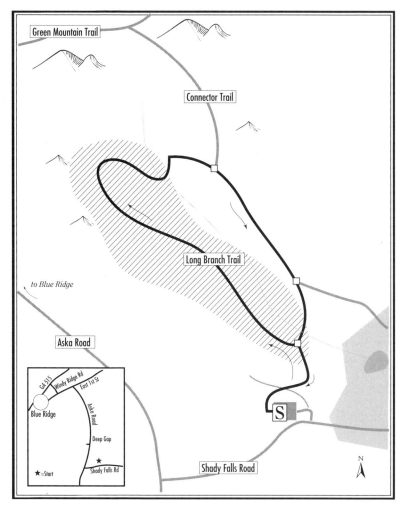

MAP KEY

Bike Route.......................... 〜

Other Trail or Road........... 〜

Direction of Travel............... →

Start/Finish............................. [S]

Milepost.................................. □

Public Land......................

Other Land......................

Recreation/Camping Area... ⛺

Major Mountain...................

River, Lake or Stream.....

Forest Service Rd. #.................. 476

Road or Trail Name..... Black Mountain Trail

Foot Travel Only....... – – ＼ ⁀ ＼ ⁀ ·

Timber Cut or Clearing.. ////

Elevation Change

2020'
1920'   1880'

④
Wahsega

You may see some of the Army Rangers from Camp Frank Merrill training as you pass their camp early in the ride. Be prepared to ford two streams, climb a couple of short but steep hills and pass through a beautiful section of forest.

Start/Finish

From US Army Camp Frank Merrill take FS 28 south 1.7 miles to where the road crosses the Etowah River. There's parking and camp spots on the road upstream along the river.

Trail Configuration

Loop with extension

Surface

Forest road • 8.5 miles

Highlights

US Army Ranger camp, stream crossings, short steep pitches, washouts

Total Distance

8.5 miles

Time Allowance

Beginner • 2 hours
Intermediate • 1.5 hours
Advanced • 1 hour

Mileposts

- **From start**– ride north on FS 28 toward Camps Wahsega and Frank Merrill.
- **Mile 0.7**– pass 4-H Camp Wahsega.
- **Mile 1.5**– turn left at US Army Camp Frank Merrill gymnasium onto FS 141. Continue down across Etowah River and past landing field.
- **Mile 2.2**– road forks. Bear left downhill on FS 141.
- **Mile 7.5**– turn left onto FS 28.
- **Mile 8.1**– at road junction and mailboxes, bear left downhill on FS 28.
- **Mile 8.5**– finish.

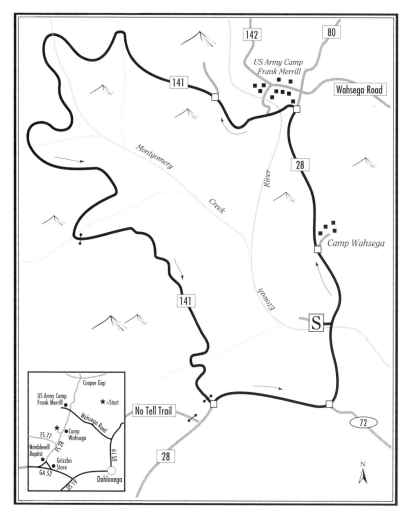

MAP KEY

Bike Route........................... ∿

Other Trail or Road........... ∿

Direction of Travel................ →

Start/Finish.............................. ⓈZ

Milepost.................................... □

Public Land......................

Other Land.......................

Recreation/Camping Area... ⛺

Major Mountain...................

River, Lake or Stream.....

Forest Service Rd. #.................. 476

Road or Trail Name..... Black Mountain Trail

Foot Travel Only.......∕ ‒ ‒ ‒ ∕ ‒ ‒ •

Timber Cut or Clearing.. ⁄⁄⁄⁄⁄

1960'

1507'

Elevation Change

⑤

Cooper Creek

As you circle Cooper Creek Scenic Area, you may begin to wonder if there is a hill around every bend. Fortunately, none are too long and the wide forest road gives you plenty of room to maneuver.

Start/Finish

Go 7.5 miles north of Suches on GA 60. Turn right onto Cooper Creek Road. Start at the junction of FS 236. Do not block the road.

Trail Configuration

Loop

Surface

Forest road • 10.8 miles
Pavement • 1.6 miles

Highlights

Recreation and scenic area, small cascades, views, rolling hills

Total Distance

12.4 miles

Time Allowance

Beginner • 2 hours
Intermediate • 1.5 hours
Advanced • 1 hour

Mileposts

- **From start**– ride toward Cooper Creek Recreation Area on FS 236.
- **Mile 2.7**– just past Cooper Creek Recreation Area, turn right onto FS 4.
- **Mile 3.5**– after passing the game check station, take the first right, which is FS 39.
- **Mile 5.6**– turn right onto FS 33A.
- **Mile 8.8**– just after crossing Cooper Creek, you'll climb a hill. Partway up, bear right onto FS 33.
- **Mile 10.8**– pavement begins. FS 33B exits to the left.
- **Mile 12.4**– finish.

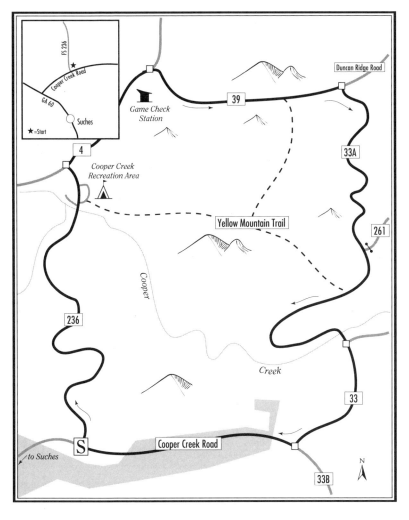

Duncan Ridge Road

FS 236

Cooper Creek Road

GA 60

Suches

★=Start

39

33A

261

Game Check Station

4

Cooper Creek Recreation Area

Yellow Mountain Trail

Cooper

236

Creek

33

S

to Suches

Cooper Creek Road

33B

N

MAP KEY

Bike Route............................	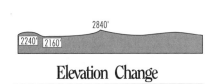	Forest Service Rd. #.................	476
Other Trail or Road...........		Road or Trail Name.....	Black Mountain Trail
Direction of Travel................	→	Foot Travel Only.......	- - -
Start/Finish............................	S	Timber Cut or Clearing..	/////
Milepost.................................	□		
Public Land......................			
Other Land.......................			
Recreation/Camping Area...	⛺	2840'	
Major Mountain...................		2240' 2160'	
River, Lake or Stream.....			

Elevation Change

Sosebee Cove

A steep descent on the highway brings you to the mouth of the cove. Soon, Slaughter Mountain looms ahead as you wind your way gradually back up, alongside Wolf Creek and through the length of the cove. The banked hairpin curves of GA 180 take you downhill back to your start at Vogel State Park.

Start/Finish

You can start inside Vogel State Park (there's a parking fee) or at the pulloff 0.6 miles down GA 180 from the park.

Trail Configuration

Loop

Surface

Forest road • 3.6 miles
Pavement • 4.2 miles

Highlights

Highway, Vogel State Park, small cascades and waterfalls, one steep uphill, steep paved downhills

Total Distance

7.8 miles

Time Allowance

Beginner • 2 hours
Intermediate • 1.25 hours
Advanced • 45 minutes

Mileposts

- **From start**– ride back to US 19/129 and turn left down the hill. Take caution on the highway.
- **Mile 2.3**– turn left onto West Wolf Creek Road.
- **Mile 2.9**– Grassy Knoll Road enters left. Emory Road enters right. Continue straight over bridge onto forest road and then bear left at top of short hill. This is FS 107.
- **Mile 3.4**– road to Wolf Creek Wilderness School enters on left. Continue straight on FS 107.
- **Mile 6.0**– steep climb up to where FS 108 enters on the right. Stay on FS 107 by bearing to the left.
- **Mile 6.5**– turn left onto GA 180. It's all downhill from here.
- **Mile 7.8**– finish.

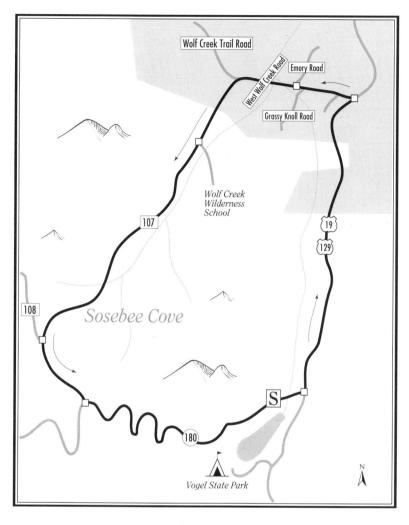

Wolf Creek Trail Road

West Wolf Creek Road

Emory Road

Grassy Knoll Road

Wolf Creek
Wilderness
School

107

108

19

129

Sosebee Cove

S

180

N

Vogel State Park

MAP KEY

Bike Route...........................	～
Other Trail or Road...........	～
Direction of Travel................	→
Start/Finish.............................	S
Milepost....................................	□
Public Land......................	
Other Land......................	
Recreation/Camping Area...	▲
Major Mountain...................	
River, Lake or Stream.....	

Forest Service Rd. #..................	476
Road or Trail Name.....	Black Mountain Trail
Foot Travel Only........	- - - -
Timber Cut or Clearing..	/////

2300'   2800'

1920'

Elevation Change

Jasus Creek

Bears! This area is heavily populated with them. The warning sign at the beginning of the ride can make you jump at the slightest sound as you travel around this gated double track loop.

Start/Finish

From Helen, drive 1 mile north on GA 17/75. Turn left onto Alt. 75. Cross river and turn right onto FS 44. Go 2.9 miles to Game Check Station. If it's hunting season, just find a convenient pulloff.

Trail Configuration

Loop w/ extension

Surface

Double track • 6.6 miles
Forest road • 5.4 miles

Highlights

Bear territory, gated-off roadway, wildlife openings, small cascades, cool streams, spotty views

Total Distance

12 miles

Time Allowance

Beginner • 2.5 hours
Intermediate • 1.75 hours
Advanced • 1.25 hours

Mileposts

- **From start–** ride north on FS 44.
- **Mile 1.2–** turn right and cross Low Gap Creek over bridge. Stay on FS 44. (FS 44A continues straight.)
- **Mile 1.6–** FS 44B enters on left. Continue on FS 44.
- **Mile 3.7–** turn left past gate onto FS 44B.
- **Mile 10.3–** a series of whoop-te-doos brings you back to FS 44. Turn right.
- **Mile 10.7–** cross Low Gap Creek and bear left.
- **Mile 12.0–** finish.

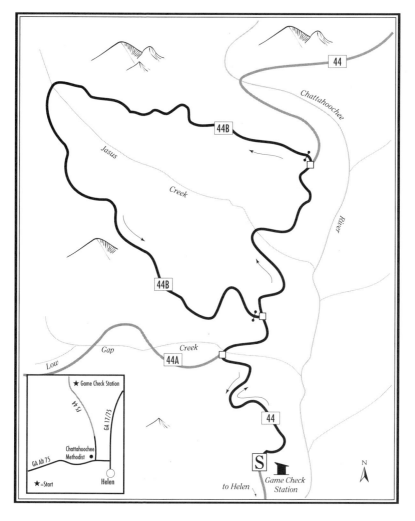

MAP KEY

Bike Route............................ 〰

Other Trail or Road............ 〰

Direction of Travel................ ⟶

Start/Finish............................ Ⓢ

Milepost................................... ▢

Public Land......................

Other Land.......................

Recreation/Camping Area... ⛺

Major Mountain....................

River, Lake or Stream.....

Forest Service Rd. #................. 476

Road or Trail Name..... Black Mountain Trail

Foot Travel Only....... ⌇

Timber Cut or Clearing.. ▨

Elevation Change

Tallulah Gorge

This is Georgia's newest state park—so new in fact, that as of the printing of this edition, facilities have yet to be completed. The summer of 1996 should see a network of trails atop the north rim of the gorge. Several of these will be designated for mountain bike use and should provide some fine riding opportunities. Be sure to call ahead or check in at the information center at the park for the latest trail updates and openings.

Location

The trails will be located in Tallulah Gorge State Park south of the Park Interpretive Center. You'll find the center atop the north rim of the gorge, just off South Rock Mountain Road.

Information

Tallulah Gorge State Park
P.O. Box 248
Tallulah Falls, GA 30573
706/754-8257

Trail Map

The map presented here shows proposed locations of both multi-use and hiking trails. The map is not intended for actual use. As the trails are completed, check with the state park information center for more specific trail, trailhead, and trail use information.

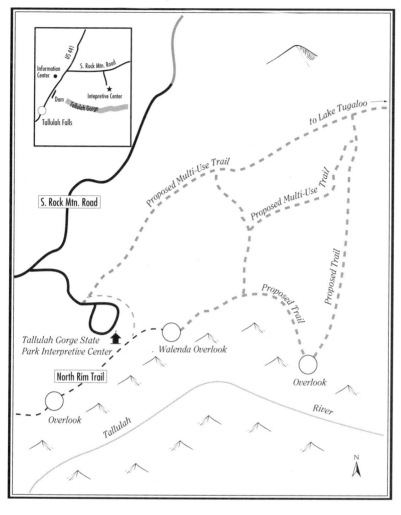

MAP KEY

Bike Route........................... ~	Forest Service Rd. #................. [476]
Other Trail or Road........... ~	Road or Trail Name..... [Black Mountain Trail]
Direction of Travel................ →	Foot Travel Only....... ‚ ⁻ ⁻ ⁻ ⁻ ⁻
Start/Finish.............................. [S]	Timber Cut or Clearing.. ////
Milepost................................... □	
Public Land...................... ▭	
Other Land....................... ▭	
Recreation/Camping Area... ⛺	
Major Mountain................... ⛰	
River, Lake or Stream..... ◣	Elevation Change

MORE DIFFICULT TRAILS

Pigeon Mountain

This flat-topped mountain with its many cliffs and caves is laced with trails. This route explores the top, which offers excellent cliff-top views, rolling terrain and many small stream crossings. Expect several short sections that are rocky, steep and difficult to ride.

Start/Finish

From LaFayette, take GA 193 north 2.8 miles and turn left on Chamberlain Road. Go 3.5 miles and turn right on Rocky Lane. Continue past the check station up the mountain (this is a rough road) 3.6 miles and turn left on East Brow Road. Go 0.25 miles to Hood Overlook to start.

Trail Configuration

Loop

Surface

Single track • 8.7 miles
Forest road • 3.7 miles

Highlights

Spectacular views; horse use; stream crossings; short steep, rocky sections; washouts; many unmarked side trails; waterfall

Total Distance

12.4 miles

Time Allowance

Beginner • 4 hours
Intermediate • 3 hours
Advanced • 2 hours

Mileposts

- **From start**– follow **orange blazed** Atwood Trail into field away from overlook.
- **Mile 0.8**– Hood Trail enters from left. Bear right.
- **Mile 1.4**– cross Rocky Lane.
- **Mile 3.8**– turn right on McCutchens Spring Road.
- **Mile 4.7**– turn left onto West Brow Trail (**white blaze**).
- **Mile 8.3**– Rape Gap. Turn left on Rocky Lane, go a few hundred yards, then right on Atwood Trail (**orange blaze**).
- **Mile 9.4**– Hood Trail exits left. Cross Allen Creek.
- **Mile 9.5**– Atwood Trail exits left. Waterfall to right. Continue straight over dirt mound onto jeep road.
- **Mile 10.7**– bear left onto East Brow Road.
- **Mile 12.4**– finish.

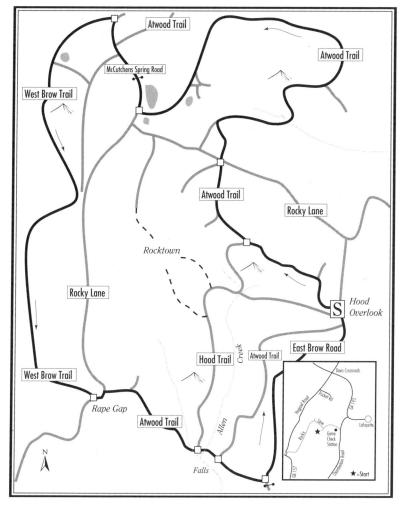

MAP KEY

Bike Route...........................	∿
Other Trail or Road...........	∿
Direction of Travel................	⟶
Start/Finish..............................	Ⓢ
Milepost...................................	▫
Public Land.......................	▭
Other Land.......................	▬
Recreation/Camping Area...	⛺
Major Mountain....................	⛰
River, Lake or Stream.....	～

Forest Service Rd. #...................	476
Road or Trail Name.....	Black Mountain Trail
Foot Travel Only.......	‧ - ‧ - ‧ - ‧
Timber Cut or Clearing..	⫽⫽⫽

Elevation Change

1970' 2130'

1590'

10

High Point

This route explores the rolling midsection of Pigeon Mountain before making the rocky climb to High Point and a spectacular cliff-top view. The ride down is across giant slabs of stone, through the woods and along the rim of the mountain.

Start/Finish

From LaFayette, take GA 193 north 2.8 miles and turn left on Chamberlain Road. Go 3.5 miles and turn right on Rocky Lane. Continue past the check station up the mountain (this is a rough road) 5 miles and turn right on McCutchens Spring Road. Start at campsite.

Trail Configuration

Loop with extension

Surface

Single track • 5 miles
Forest road • 3.3 miles

Highlights

Spectacular views, horse use, steep climb, boulders and rock slabs, short pushes

Total Distance

8.3 miles

Time Allowance

Beginner • 4 hours
Intermediate • 2.5 hours
Advanced • 1.5 hours

Mileposts

- **From start**– ride down McCutchens Spring Road out past ponds and around gate.
- **Mile 0.7**– turn right on Atwood Trail (**orange blaze**).
- **Mile 3.2**– turn left onto Atwood Point Road.
- **Mile 4.5**– turn right onto McCutchens Spring Road and continue down and around gate.
- **Mile 5**– turn left onto West Brow Trail (**blue and white double blazes**). Start hill climb.
- **Mile 6**– High Point.
- **Mile 6.8**– South Pocket Trail exits right.
- **Mile 7.1**– turn right onto McCutchens Spring Road and continue on it to the finish.
- **Mile 8.3**– finish.

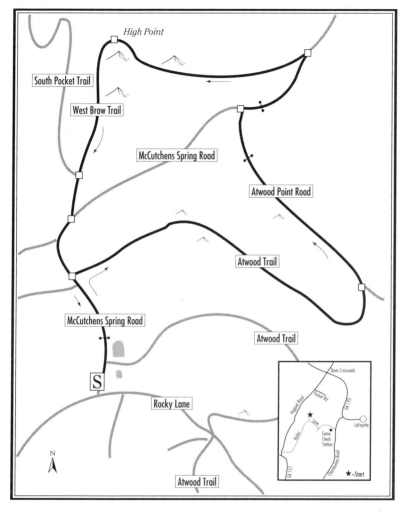

High Point

South Pocket Trail

West Brow Trail

McCutchens Spring Road

Atwood Point Road

Atwood Trail

McCutchens Spring Road

Atwood Trail

S

Rocky Lane

Atwood Trail

Davis Crossroads

Pocket Rd

GA 193

Hogjowl Road

Rocky Lane

Lafayette

Game Check Station

GA 157

Chamberlain Road

★ = Start

N

MAP KEY

Bike Route.......................... ∿	Forest Service Rd. #................. 476
Other Trail or Road........... ∿	Road or Trail Name..... Black Mountain Trail
Direction of Travel................ →	Foot Travel Only....... ⌇ ⌇ ⌇
Start/Finish............................. S	Timber Cut or Clearing.. ⫽⫽⫽
Milepost.................................. □	
Public Land....................... ▭	
Other Land....................... ▮	
Recreation/Camping Area... ⛺	
Major Mountain.................... ⛰	2001' 2329'
River, Lake or Stream..... ᝰ	1322'

Elevation Change

11

Iron Mountain

The single track portion of this trail winds and twists along the side of Iron Mountain while a forest road takes you to an old tower site with spectacular views. Be sure to take the alternate high-water route at the beginning if the river is up to avoid being swept away.

Start/Finish

From Cisco, on US 411, take Old GA 2 eight miles to Cottonwood Patch Campground to start.

Trail Configuration

Loop with extension

Surface

Single track • 4.1 miles
Forest road • 6.9 miles

Highlights

Spectacular view, horse use, river crossing, twisty single track

Total Distance

11 miles

Time Allowance

Beginner • 2.5 hours
Intermediate • 1.5 hours
Advanced • 1 hour

Mileposts

- **From start**– ride along river and out back of campground. *Alternate start: If the river is running high, go back the way you drove in, cross the bridge, turn right on the forest road and ride downstream to the river crossing.*
- **Mile 0.3**– ford the Conasauga River.
- **Mile 4.1**– turn right onto FS 1.
- **Mile 4.9**– road exits right, bear left.
- **Mile 5.5**– old lookout site. Turn around.
- **Mile 6.1**– pass road exiting to left.
- **Mile 6.9**– pass entrance to Iron Mountain Trail.
- **Mile 8**– turn left onto Old GA 2.
- **Mile 11**– finish.

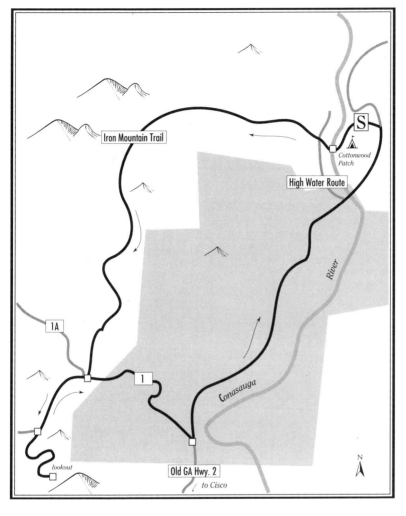

MAP KEY

Bike Route..........................

Other Trail or Road...........

Direction of Travel...............

Start/Finish............................ S

Milepost.................................. □

Public Land......................

Other Land......................

Recreation/Camping Area... ⛺

Major Mountain..................

River, Lake or Stream.....

Forest Service Rd. #................. 476

Road or Trail Name..... Black Mountain Trail

Foot Travel Only.......

Timber Cut or Clearing..

1000'   2032'

Elevation Change

12

Bear Creek

The single track on this trail is just technical enough to test your skills, while riding across and alongside the stream is beautiful. You'll also pass the immense Gennett Poplar.

Start/Finish

From milepost 8 on GA 52 west of Ellijay, take County Road #65 north for 5.4 miles. Continue onto FS 90 for another 1.7 miles, turn right on FS 68 and go 2 miles to the trailhead parking area.

Trail Configuration

Loop

Surface

Single/double track • 9.6 miles
Forest road • 0.5 miles

Highlights

Woods roads, whoop-te-doos, great views, stream crossings, Gennett Poplar, one very steep uphill, wildlife openings

Total Distance

10.1 miles

Time Allowance

Beginner • 2.25 hours
Intermediate • 1.5 hours
Advanced • 1.25 hours

Mileposts

- **From start**– ride out back of parking area onto trail.
- **Mile 0.4**– turn left onto Barnes Creek Road.
- **Mile 1.8**– turn right past gate onto Bear Creek Trail.
- **Mile 2.1**– at wildlife opening, turn left over whoop-te-doo.
- **Mile 3.4**– Bear Creek Loop sign marks trail to left. Continue straight down the creek past Gennett Poplar.
- **Mile 4.4**– lower trailhead. Go 200 feet and trail continues on left side of road. Look for the **blue blazes**.
- **Mile 4.9**– turn left onto grassy roadbed.
- **Mile 5.3**– go left at fork following **blue blazed posts**.
- **Mile 6.0**– Bear Creek Loop sign marks trail to left. Continue to the right.
- **Mile 8.3**– pass Bear Creek Trail sign on left.
- **Mile 9.6**– pass trail to parking lot, then turn right past gate onto FS 68.
- **Mile 10.1**– finish.

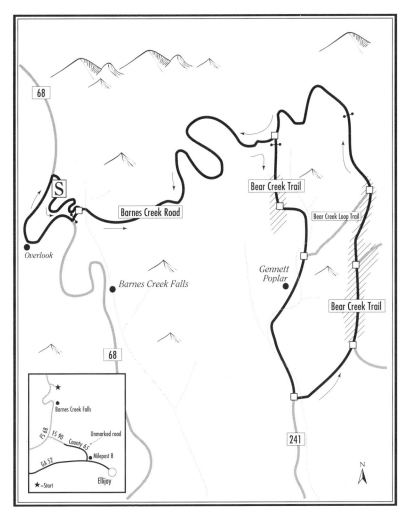

68

S

Barnes Creek Road

Overlook

Barnes Creek Falls

Bear Creek Trail

Bear Creek Loop Trail

Gennett
Poplar

Bear Creek Trail

68

241

Barnes Creek Falls

FS 68   FS 90   Unmarked road
County 65
Milepost 8
GA 52   Ellijay
★ =Start

N

MAP KEY

Bike Route.........................
Other Trail or Road...........
Direction of Travel.................
Start/Finish............................ $\boxed{S}$
Milepost.................................. □
Public Land......................
Other Land......................
Recreation/Camping Area... ⛺
Major Mountain...................
River, Lake or Stream.....

Forest Service Rd. #................. $\boxed{476}$
Road or Trail Name..... $\boxed{\text{Black Mountain Trail}}$
Foot Travel Only........
Timber Cut or Clearing..

2800'
1760'

Elevation Change

13

Tatum Lead

A real teeth-rattler at times, this route follows the ridgeline of Tatum Mountain out and back. The steep, whoop-te-doo-filled side loop on the far end will definitely get your attention.

Start/Finish

One mile east of Cohutta Lodge on GA 52 at the entrance to Tatum Lead Road. *There is very limited parking here so you may want to ask permission and park at the lodge.*

Trail Configuration

Out-and-back w/ loop extension

Surface

Single/double track • 7.3 miles
Forest Road • 7.2 miles

Highlights

Steep uphill and downhill, rocky trail, whoop-te-doos, spotty views, ATV and ORV use

Total Distance

14.5 miles

Time Allowance

Beginner • 3.5 hours
Intermediate • 2.5 hours
Advanced • 1.75 hours

Mileposts

- **From start**– ride south on Tatum Lead Road. This road starts out as a right of way across private land.
- **Mile 0.8**– you'll pass a gated road on the right and a little farther along, another road on the left. Continue straight on at each junction.
- **Mile 0.9**– a road goes downhill to the right. Stay left.
- **Mile 1.8**– Forest Service boundary. Just past where a jeep road turns off to the left, the road forks. Go right.
- **Mile 5**– turn right onto Rock Creek ATV Loop Trail.
- **Mile 6.4**– turn left (uphill) at ATV loop sign.
- **Mile 8.4**– turn left back onto Tatum Lead Road.
- **Mile 9.1**– pass turnoff to Rock Creek ATV Loop Trail.
- **Mile 14.5**– continue past previous mileposts to finish.

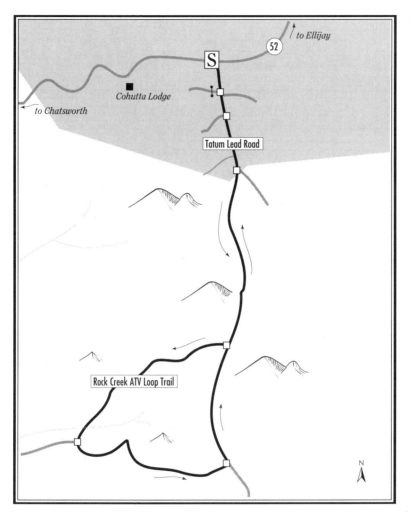

52

to Ellijay

S

Cohutta Lodge

to Chatsworth

Tatum Lead Road

Rock Creek ATV Loop Trail

N

MAP KEY

Bike Route........................... 〰

Other Trail or Road........... 〰

Direction of Travel................ ⟶

Start/Finish............................. Ⓢ

Milepost.................................. ☐

Public Land......................

Other Land.......................

Recreation/Camping Area... ⛺

Major Mountain...................

River, Lake or Stream.....

Forest Service Rd. #.................. 476

Road or Trail Name..... Black Mountain Trail

Foot Travel Only....... ⌐ ⌐ ⌐ ⌐

Timber Cut or Clearing.. ⫽⫽⫽

2840'

2600'

1750'

Elevation Change

14

Carters Lake

This fun all-single-track loop follows the contours of the low ridges alongside Carters Lake. You'll find numerous short, steep ups and downs as well as plenty of twists and turns through the woods. There are plenty of side trails, but the main trail is well marked and easy to follow.

Start/Finish

Ridgeway Recreation Area boat ramp parking area on Carters Lake west of Ellijay off US 76.

Trail Configuration

Loop

Surface

Single track • 5.6 miles

Highlights

Views of lake, steep sections, easy to follow, very twisty

Total Distance

5.6 miles

Time Allowance

Beginner • 2.5 hours
Intermediate • 1.5 hours
Advanced • 1 hour

Mileposts

- **From start**– ride out between men's and women's outhouses following the **orange posts**. You will do the loop counterclockwise
- **Mile 0.8**– bear right just before road.
- **Mile 1.1**– trail from road enters from left. Bear right.
- **Mile 2.2**– turn right onto spur to scenic view.
- **Mile 2.3**– scenic view. Turn around and continue back past last milepost onto loop.
- **Mile 2.4**– at toilets, make hard right downhill.
- **Mile 3.5**– trail splits. You can go either way.
- **Mile 4.2**– cross road. A little farther up, a woods road will enter from the right.
- **Mile 5.6**– finish.

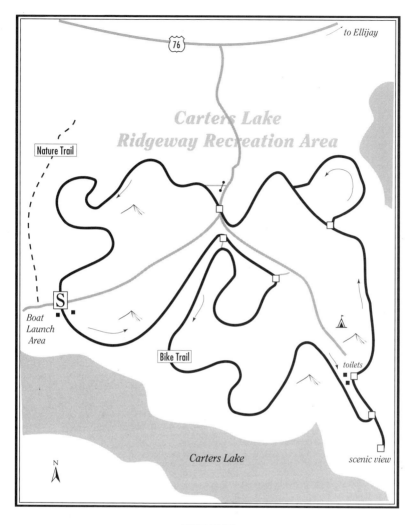

to Ellijay

76

Carters Lake
Ridgeway Recreation Area

Nature Trail

S

Boat
Launch
Area

Bike Trail

toilets

scenic view

N

Carters Lake

MAP KEY

Bike Route...........................	〜
Other Trail or Road...........	〜
Direction of Travel...............	⟶
Start/Finish............................	S
Milepost....................................	□
Public Land.......................	▭
Other Land.......................	▭
Recreation/Camping Area...	⛺
Major Mountain..................	⛰
River, Lake or Stream.....	

Forest Service Rd. #..................	476
Road or Trail Name.....	Black Mountain Trail
Foot Travel Only........	- ~ - ~ -
Timber Cut or Clearing..	///////

1370'

1100'

Elevation Change

15

South Fork

This is the only chance you get to ride alongside the Jacks River before it plunges into the Cohutta Wilderness. Wildlife openings make room for terrific views of the ridges above and you can plan on getting wet feet at the stream crossings.

Start/Finish

From Blue Ridge, take GA 5 north for 3.7 miles, turn left on Old GA 2 and continue another 10.5 miles to Watson Gap. *Alternate start: Jacks River Fields. There's better parking, but you have to drive another 4 miles on rough FS 64.*

Trail Configuration

Loop

Surface

Single track • 2.7 miles
Forest road • 5.4 miles

Highlights

Stream crossings, lush, boggy areas, small mountain community, nice views

Total Distance

8.1 miles

Time Allowance

Beginner • 2 hours
Intermediate • 1.5 hours
Advanced • 1 hour

Mileposts

- **From start**– at Watson Gap, go south on FS 64.
- **Mile 3.2**– Dyer Gap. FS 64A exits to left. Stay on FS 64.
- **Mile 3.8**– at bottom of hill and just before crossing Jacks River, turn right onto South Fork Trail.
- **Mile 4.4**– Benton Mackaye Trail enters from right. It has a **white diamond blaze**.
- **Mile 6**– Benton Mackaye Trail exits to right. Continue on South Fork Trail.
- **Mile 6.5**– cross dirt mound onto woods road.
- **Mile 6.7**– ford river, ride up hill and turn right on FS 126.
- **Mile 7.4**– Jones Settlement. Continue straight on FS 126.
- **Mile 8.1**– finish.

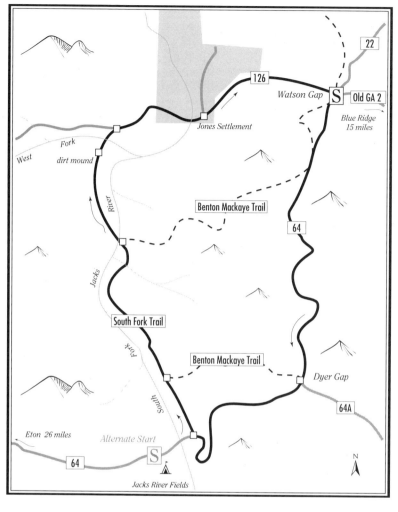

22

126

Watson Gap S Old GA 2

Jones Settlement

Blue Ridge
15 miles

Fork

West

dirt mound

River

Benton Mackaye Trail

64

Jacks

South Fork Trail

Fork

Benton Mackaye Trail

Dyer Gap

South

64A

Eton 26 miles

Alternate Start

64 S

N

Jacks River Fields

MAP KEY

Bike Route..........................	Forest Service Rd. #.................	476
Other Trail or Road...........	Road or Trail Name.....	Black Mountain Trail
Direction of Travel................	Foot Travel Only........	
Start/Finish.............................. S		
Milepost.................................... □		
Public Land........................	Timber Cut or Clearing..	
Other Land........................		
Recreation/Camping Area...		
Major Mountain....................		
River, Lake or Stream.....		

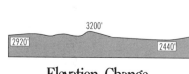

3200'

2920' 2440'

Elevation Change

16

Green Mountain

You start out with a choice of how to get to the top of Green Mountain. One is hard; the other is not so hard. From the top, it's a downhill rush to the shores of Lake Blue Ridge on terrific single track. Be prepared for a long climb at the end.

Start/Finish

From GA 515 on the north side of Blue Ridge, take Windy Ridge Road 0.1 miles south, turn left on E 1st Street, go 0.1 miles and turn right on Aska Road. It's 3.5 miles to the Deep Gap trailhead.

Trail Configuration

Loop

Surface

Single track • 3.4 miles
Forest road • 2.2 miles
Pavement • 1.9 miles

Highlights

Long downhill on single track, well marked, lake views, vacation homes, uphill to finish

Total Distance

7.5 miles

Time Allowance

Beginner • 2 hours
Intermediate • 1.5 hours
Advanced • 1 hour

Mileposts

- **From start–** cross Aska Road onto either one of the **white blazed** Green Mountain Trails (the upper trail is hard and steep). They connect at the one mile point.
- **Mile 1.6–** connector trail to Long Branch exits right.
- **Mile 2.2–** old roadbed enters from right. Bear left.
- **Mile 2.3–** take a sharp right off old roadbed and cross small stream. Lake Blue Ridge will be to your right.
- **Mile 3.4–** Lower Green Mountain Trail trailhead. Continue straight onto FS 711.
- **Mile 4.7–** turn left at T-intersection.
- **Mile 4.9–** turn right onto Campbell Camp Road.
- **Mile 5.6–** turn left onto Aska Road.
- **Mile 7.5–** finish.

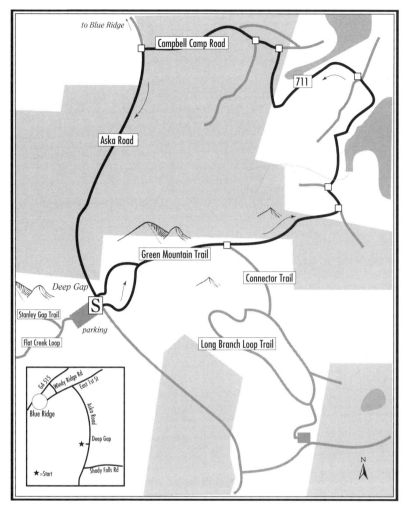

Campbell Camp Road

711

Aska Road

Green Mountain Trail

Deep Gap

Connector Trail

S

Stanley Gap Trail

parking

Flat Creek Loop

Long Branch Loop Trail

Ga 515

Windy Ridge Rd

East 1st St

Blue Ridge

Aska Road

Deep Gap

★ =Start

Shady Falls Rd

N

MAP KEY

Bike Route...........................	〜	Forest Service Rd. #.................	476
Other Trail or Road...........	〜	Road or Trail Name.....	Black Mountain Trail
Direction of Travel................	→	Foot Travel Only........	- - - - - -
Start/Finish............................	S	Timber Cut or Clearing..	/////
Milepost...................................	□		
Public Land.......................	▭		
Other Land.......................	▬		
Recreation/Camping Area...	▲		
Major Mountain...................	⛰		
River, Lake or Stream.....	〰		

2520'

2120'

1680'

Elevation Change

17

Stanley Gap

Fabulous single track makes this one heck of a trail! On this route, a paved downhill takes you to the Toccoa River before going up, up, up on a forest road to the trail. You then ride over the top of the mountain and along the ridge on sweet single track.

Start/Finish

From GA 515 on the north side of Blue Ridge, take Windy Ridge Road 0.1 miles south, turn left on E 1st Street, go 0.1 miles and turn right on Aska Road. It's 3.5 miles to the Deep Gap trailhead.

Trail Configuration

Loop

Surface

Single track • 4.9 miles
Forest road • 3.9 miles
Pavement • 3.7 miles

Highlights

Views, long rocky downhill, river rapids, vacation homes, small stream crossings

Total Distance

12.5 miles

Time Allowance

Beginner • 3 hours
Intermediate • 2.25 hours
Advanced • 1.5 hours

Mileposts

- **From start**– turn right from trailhead parking area, downhill on Aska Road.
- **Mile 3.7**– turn right onto Stanley Gap Road. It's marked by a sign for Rich Mountain WMA. (Toccoa River Outpost is on the left.)
- **Mile 7.6**– Stanley Gap and Stanley Gap trailhead. Turn right onto Stanley Gap Trail. (**white blazes**).
- **Mile 8.2**– Benton Mackaye Trail enters right.
- **Mile 10.1**– Benton Mackaye Trail exits left.
- **Mile 11.9**– Flat Creek Connector Trail continues straight ahead. Turn left to stay on Stanley Gap Trail.
- **Mile 12.5**– bear left at trail junction to finish.

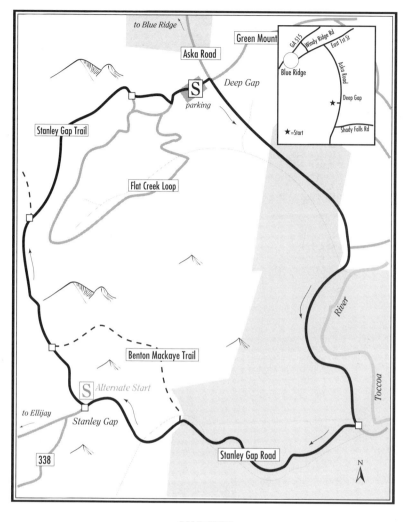

to Blue Ridge

Green Mount

Aska Road

S Deep Gap

parking

Stanley Gap Trail

Flat Creek Loop

GA 515
Windy Ridge Rd
East 1st St
Blue Ridge
Aska Road
Deep Gap
★ = Start
Shady Falls Rd

River

Toccoa

Benton Mackaye Trail

S Alternate Start

to Ellijay

Stanley Gap

338

Stanley Gap Road

N

MAP KEY

Bike Route...........................

Other Trail or Road............

Direction of Travel................

Start/Finish.............................. S

Milepost.................................... □

Public Land......................

Other Land........................

Recreation/Camping Area... ⛺

Major Mountain..................

River, Lake or Stream.....

Forest Service Rd. #................. 476

Road or Trail Name..... Black Mountain Trail

Foot Travel Only........

Timber Cut or Clearing..

2120'   3442'

1720'

Elevation Change

18

Flat Creek

You'll gradually climb to the head of Flat Creek before turning back down through the cove. Expect small stream crossings, tunnels of rhododendron and to slip-slide through baseball-sized rocks. It's a steep climb back to the start of the loop.

Start/Finish

From GA 515 on the north side of Blue Ridge, take Windy Ridge Road 0.1 miles south, turn left on E 1st Street, go 0.1 miles and turn right on Aska Road. It's 3.5 miles to the Deep Gap trailhead.

Trail Configuration

Loop

Surface

Single/double track • 5.6 miles

Highlights

Stream crossings, rhododendron tunnels, rocky section, steep but ridable uphill

Total Distance

5.6 miles

Time Allowance

Beginner • 2 hours
Intermediate • 1.5 hours
Advanced • 1 hour

Mileposts

- **From start**– ride out back of trailhead parking area.
- **Mile 0.1**– trail forks. Bear left onto Flat Creek Trail. It's marked with **green and white dot blazes**.
- **Mile 0.5**– bear right on double track to begin loop.
- **Mile 0.6**– Stanley Gap Connector Trail exits right. Stay on Flat Creek Trail.
- **Mile 3**– several abandoned woods roads enter and exit trail. Stay on Flat Creek Trail.
- **Mile 4**– turn left off double track onto single track, cross Flat Creek and bear left upstream.
- **Mile 5.1**– after steep climb, end loop and bear right.
- **Mile 5.5**– Stanley Gap Trail enters from left.
- **Mile 5.6**– finish.

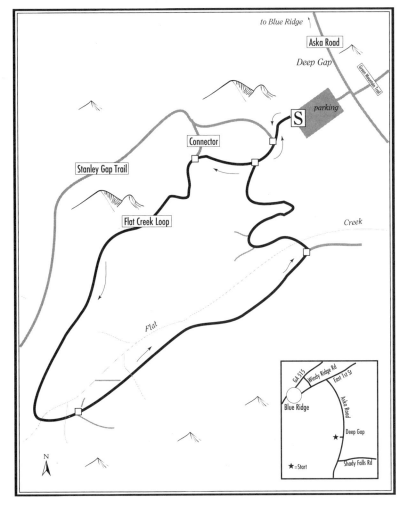

MAP KEY

Bike Route...........................

Other Trail or Road...........

Direction of Travel................ →

Start/Finish.............................. ⑤

Milepost................................... □

Public Land......................

Other Land......................

Recreation/Camping Area... 🏕

Major Mountain...................

River, Lake or Stream.....

Forest Service Rd. #.................. 476

Road or Trail Name..... Black Mountain Trail

Foot Travel Only....... ⌐ ‑ ⌐ ⌐ ‑

Timber Cut or Clearing.. ////////

Elevation Change

2800'

2120'

1980'

19

River Loop

This technical route alongside the Cartecay River packs a lot of punch. Take it easy on the hill down to the water's edge—it's very steep. You may want to connect this with the Red and White Loop for a longer ride.

Start/Finish

From GA 515 in Ellijay, take GA 52 east for 3.2 miles and turn right onto County Road 225. Go 0.4 miles and turn right into the Rich Mountain WMA Cartecay Tract. Go 0.3 miles to start at the gate.

Trail Configuration

Loop

Surface

Single track • 2.3 miles
Forest road • 1.1 miles

Highlights

Great single track, one extremely steep downhill, Cartecay River, rapids, beaches, boggy areas, technical riding

Total Distance

3.4 miles

Time Allowance

Beginner • 1 hour
Intermediate • 45 minutes
Advanced • 30 minutes

Mileposts

- **From start**– ride past gate out gravel road.
- **Mile 0.1**– Red and White Loop enters from right at the gate. Bear left.
- **Mile 0.2**– small clearing with hidden trail entering on right. Begin loop by bearing left on the road.
- **Mile 0.7**– turnaround area with gated road entering on left. Continue across onto **white blazed** trail.
- **Mile 1.2**– steep downhill to river.
- **Mile 3.0**– Red & White Loop Trail enters from left. Stay straight unless you want to combine the loops.
- **Mile 3.1**– Cross dirt barricade and bear left onto road.
- **Mile 3.2**– pass gate to Red & White Loop.
- **Mile 3.4**– finish.

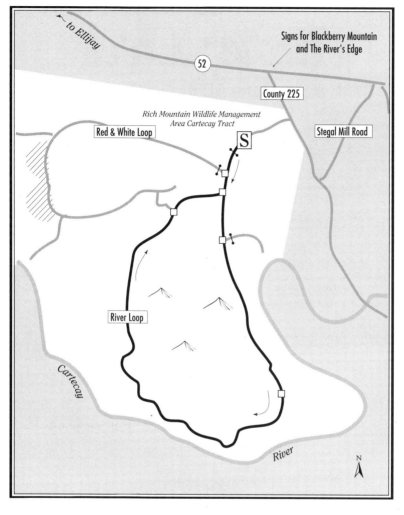

MAP KEY

Bike Route.........................

Other Trail or Road...........

Direction of Travel................ ⟶

Start/Finish............................. Ⓢ

Milepost................................... □

Public Land.......................

Other Land.......................

Recreation/Camping Area... ⛺

Major Mountain...................

River, Lake or Stream.....

Forest Service Rd. #.................. 476

Road or Trail Name..... Black Mountain Trail

Foot Travel Only....... ⟋ ‒ ﹀ ⟍ ﹀ ⟋ ⟍ ﹀

Timber Cut or Clearing.. ⧄

1600'   1648'

1360'

Elevation Change

20

Turner Creek

The abandoned woods roads of No Tell Trail loop you up and around and finally to the top of Turner Creek. Here the trail tightens up as it twists and turns down alongside and over the small stream that gives it its name

Start/Finish

From Nimblewill Baptist Church off GA 52 near Dahlonega, go 2.9 miles on FS 28 and start at end of Turner Creek Trail. *A biker parking lot is planned in the area. If it is finished, start there.*

Trail Configuration

Loop

Surface

Single track • 2.9 miles
Forest road • 2.4 miles

Highlights

Horse use, steep section, wooden bridges, tight single track

Total Distance

5.3 miles

Time Allowance

Beginner • 1.5 hours
Intermediate • 1 hour
Advanced • 45 minutes

Mileposts

- **From start–** ride north on FS 28.
- **Mile 0.6–** FS 28A enters from left. Stay on FS 28.
- **Mile 1.1–** turn left around gate onto No Tell Trail.
- **Mile 1.7–** old woods road/trail enters from the left. Bear right.
- **Mile 1.9–** trail forks. Bear left down the hill.
- **Mile 2.5–** turn right onto FS 28A.
- **Mile 3.3–** just before road junctions with FS 77, turn left down Turner Creek Trail.
- **Mile 4.8–** trail forks. Horses only to right. Bikes to left. Go left down across bridge.
- **Mile 5.3–** finish.

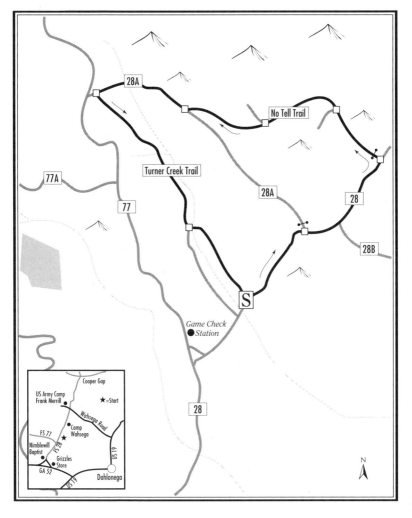

MAP KEY

Bike Route...........................	∿
Other Trail or Road...........	∿
Direction of Travel................	→
Start/Finish............................	⑤
Milepost..................................	□
Public Land........................	▭
Other Land........................	▬
Recreation/Camping Area...	⛺
Major Mountain....................	⛰
River, Lake or Stream.....	

Forest Service Rd. #.................	476
Road or Trail Name.....	Black Mountain Trail
Foot Travel Only.......	～ ‑ ～ ‑ ～ ‑
Timber Cut or Clearing..	/////

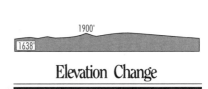

Elevation Change

21

Winding Stair

This is forest road ridge-riding at its best. After a long climb, you'll cruise around the tops of some of Georgia's highest peaks for over 7 miles and pass through 9 gaps. From the last, Winding Stair Gap, you'll make a 4-mile plunge to the finish.

Start/Finish

From Nimblewill Baptist Church off GA 52 near Dahlonega, go 2.2 miles on FS 28 and start at the junction of FS 77. *A biker parking lot is planned in the area. If it is finished, start there.*

Trail Configuration

Loop

Surface

Forest road • 19.3 miles

Highlights

Ridge-riding, views, rocky roadbed, long climb, long descent, Army Ranger camp

Total Distance

19.3 miles

Time Allowance

Beginner • 4.5 hours
Intermediate • 3.25 hours
Advanced • 2 hours

Mileposts

- **From start–** ride north on FS 28.
- **Mile 2.5–** roads jct. at mailboxes. Stay on FS 28.
- **Mile 4.2–** pass US Army Camp Frank Merrill and continue across pavement onto FS 80. Begin long climb to Cooper Gap.
- **Mile 7–** Cooper Gap. Turn left onto FS 42. **Do not ride on Appalachian Trail**.
- **Mile 10.6–** FS 69 enters from right. Stay on FS 42.
- **Mile 14.4–** Winding Stair Gap. Big intersection of roads. Turn left, downhill onto FS 77.
- **Mile 19.3–** finish.

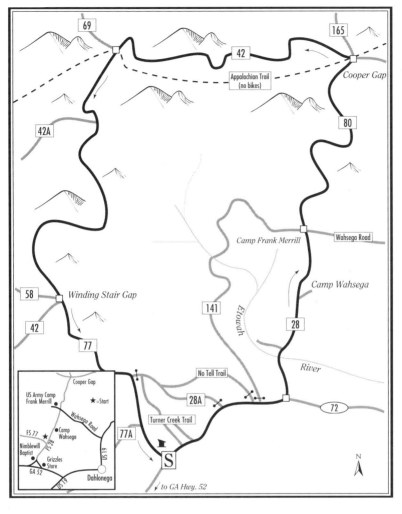

MAP KEY

Bike Route...........................	(symbol)
Other Trail or Road...........	(symbol)
Direction of Travel...............	→
Start/Finish..........................	S
Milepost...............................	□
Public Land........................	(box)
Other Land.........................	(shaded box)
Recreation/Camping Area...	⛺
Major Mountain...................	(symbol)
River, Lake or Stream.....	(symbol)

Forest Service Rd. #.................	476
Road or Trail Name.....	Black Mountain Trail
Foot Travel Only........	- - ⌐ - ⌐ -
Timber Cut or Clearing..	/////

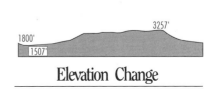

Elevation Change

1800'
3257'
1507'

22

Canada Creek

It seems as if this ride is constantly going downhill (you pay later) while you work your way from where the Appalachian Trail crosses the high ridges. You'll find a hidden single track surprise as you traverse Canada Creek Road over to Pleasant Valley.

Start/Finish

From downtown Dahlonega, go 2.2 miles north on GA 60. Turn left on Wahsega Road. Go 8.5 miles and turn right onto FS 80 at Camp Frank Merrill. Go 2.8 miles to Cooper Gap to start.

Trail Configuration

Loop

Surface

Single track • 0.8 miles
Forest road • 11.4 miles
Pavement • 2.6 miles

Highlights

Great views, lots of downhill, old farm houses, stream crossing, streams, loose gravel

Total Distance

14.8 miles

Time Allowance

Beginner • 3 hours
Intermediate • 2 hours
Advanced • 1.25 hours

Mileposts

- **From start**– ride east on FS 42 towards Suches. **Do not ride on Appalachian Trail.**
- **Mile 7.0**– turn left onto gravel Canada Creek Road. It looks like a driveway. Continue up past houses.
- **Mile 7.6**– road forks. Bear right.
- **Mile 9.3**– road closed barricade and an old washed out wooden bridge. Ford Canada Creek and go over dirt barricades up the grassy roadbed turned single track.
- **Mile 10.1**– cross over dirt barricade and bear left.
- **Mile 10.4**– road enters from left. Bear right past houses.
- **Mile 11.3**– turn left onto Gaddistown Road.
- **Mile 14.8**– finish.

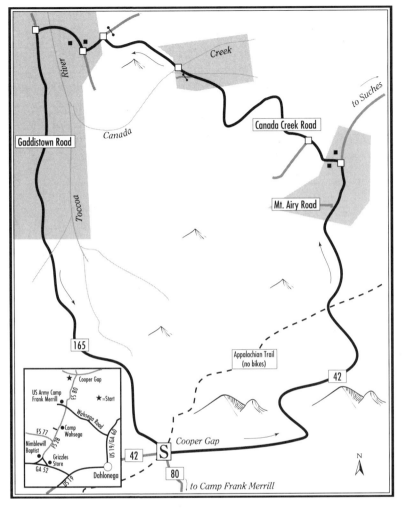

Creek

to Suches

Canada Creek Road

Gaddistown Road

Canada

Mt. Airy Road

Toccoa

River

165

Appalachian Trail
(no bikes)

42

Cooper Gap

US Army Camp
Frank Merrill

★ =Start

FS 80

Wahsega Road

FS 77

Camp
Wahsega

FS 28

Nimblewill
Baptist

Grizzles
Store

GA 52

US 19

Dahlonega

US 19/GA 60

42

S

80

to Camp Frank Merrill

N

MAP KEY

Bike Route...........................

Other Trail or Road...........

Direction of Travel.................

Start/Finish.............................. $\boxed{S}$

Milepost..................................... □

Public Land......................

Other Land.......................

Recreation/Camping Area... ⛺

Major Mountain...................

River, Lake or Stream.....

Forest Service Rd. #................. $\boxed{476}$

Road or Trail Name..... Black Mountain Trail

Foot Travel Only........ - - - -

Timber Cut or Clearing..

2820'   2991'

2120'

Elevation Change

Duncan Ridge

23

Starting with a fast descent to Lake Winfield Scott, this ride goes down, down, down for close to 10 miles before a steady climb up and onto Duncan Ridge. It's then a ridgeline ride on a rough road to the finish.

Start/Finish

From Vogel State Park, go 3.5 miles on GA 180 to its jct. with Duncan Ridge Road. Start here.

Trail Configuration

Loop

Surface

Forest road • 16.3 miles
Pavement • 4.2 miles

Highlights

Long, fast, swooping downhill on pavement, rocky roads, views

Total Distance

20.5 miles

Time Allowance

Beginner • 3 hours
Intermediate • 2.5 hours
Advanced • 1.75 hours

Mileposts

- **From start–** ride (downhill) on GA 180.
- **Mile 2.7–** Lake Winfield Scott on left.
- **Mile 3.3–** turn right onto Cooper Creek Road. 0.3 miles down the road will be a sign for Cooper Creek Wildlife Management Area.
- **Mile 4.2–** pavement ends and gravel FS 33 begins. Stay on this road for the next 5.6 miles.
- **Mile 9.8–** bear right onto FS 33A. Go downhill and cross Cooper Creek on a bridge.
- **Mile 11.6–** FS 261 exits right. Stay on FS 33A.
- **Mile 13.0–** junction Duncan Ridge Road (FS 39). Turn right.
- **Mile 13.4–** road exits right. Stay left on Duncan Ridge Road and continue to climb up the ridge.
- **Mile 20.5–** finish.

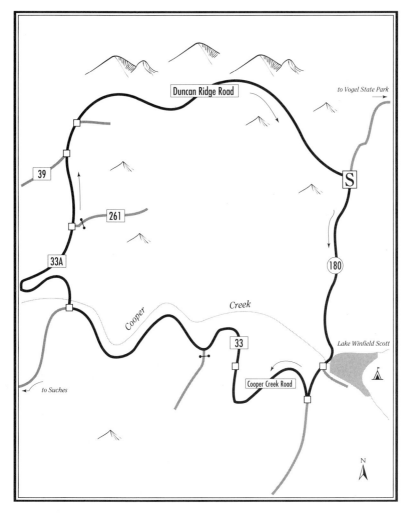

Duncan Ridge Road

to Vogel State Park

39

261

33A

S

180

Cooper Creek

33

Lake Winfield Scott

Cooper Creek Road

to Suches

N

MAP KEY

Bike Route.........................	
Other Trail or Road..........	
Direction of Travel...............	
Start/Finish............................	S
Milepost..................................	□
Public Land......................	
Other Land......................	
Recreation/Camping Area...	
Major Mountain..................	
River, Lake or Stream.....	

Forest Service Rd. #.................	476
Road or Trail Name.....	Black Mountain Trail
Foot Travel Only.......	
Timber Cut or Clearing..	

3280'   3750'

2360'

Elevation Change

24

Upper Hooch

This route circles the upper reaches of the Chattahoochee River north of Helen. Be prepared to do some climbing on the far end of the loop. It's worth it, as your legs will soon get a *break* while your *brakes* get a workout as you spin your way back down to the river.

Start/Finish

From Helen, drive 1 mile north on GA 17/75. Turn left on Alt. 75. Cross river and turn right on FS 44. Go 2.9 miles to Game Check Station. If it's hunting season, skip the check station and find a convenient pulloff.

Trail Configuration

Loop

Surface

Forest road • 15.4 miles

Highlights

Chattahoochee River, small waterfalls, great views, timber cuts, wildlife openings, river ford

Total Distance

15.4 miles

Time Allowance

Beginner • 3 hours
Intermediate • 2.25 hours
Advanced • 1.5 hours

Mileposts

- **From start**– ride north on FS 44.
- **Mile 1.2**– bear right across Low Gap Creek.
- **Mile 1.7**– FS 44B enters from left. Stay on FS 44.
- **Mile 3.7**– the other end of FS 44B enters from left.
- **Mile 5.3**– FS 44C enters from left. Stay on FS 44..
- **Mile 6.6**– FS 44E enters from left. Stay on FS 44.
- **Mile 9.4**– turn right past gate onto FS 178.
- **Mile 12.6**– continue past gate.
- **Mile 13.7**– gated road enters from left. Bear right.
- **Mile 14.7**– ford river and turn right onto FS 44.
- **Mile 15.4**– finish.

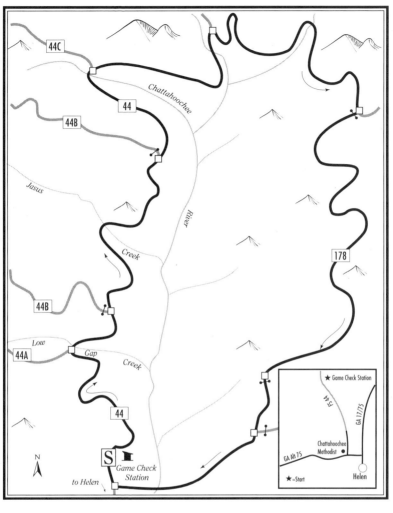

MAP KEY

Bike Route............................ 〰

Other Trail or Road............ 〰

Direction of Travel................ →

Start/Finish............................. Ⓢ

Milepost.................................... □

Public Land.........................

Other Land.........................

Recreation/Camping Area... ⛺

Major Mountain....................

River, Lake or Stream.....

Forest Service Rd. #................. 476

Road or Trail Name..... Black Mountain Trail

Foot Travel Only........ - - - - -

Timber Cut or Clearing.. ////

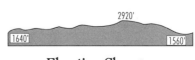

Elevation Change

25

Helen

Much of this well marked trail is used as part of the big NORBA Nationals Race held each year. Don't let the distance fool you, this is a tough ride. It's also a lot of fun with its twists and turns and stream crossings.

Start/Finish
Municipal parking lot on Chattahoochee Street, just past the visitors center in Helen.

Trail Configuration
Loop

Surface
Single track • 6.1 miles
Pavement • 0.3 mile

Highlights
Short steep hills, short pushes stream crossings, many side trails, roots, washouts

Total Distance
6.4 miles

Time Allowance
Beginner • 2 hours
Intermediate • 1.5 hours
Advanced • 1 hour

Mileposts

- **From start**– ride north, up Chattahoochee Street.
- **Mile 0.1**– just before hairpin turn, turn left onto bike trail and then take the right fork up the steep hill.
- **Mile 1.3**– turn left onto old woods road.
- **Mile 1.9**– cross Volksmarch Trail and then turn right down the side of the mountain.
- **Mile 2.2**– turn right, cross creek, then right again.
- **Mile 2.4**– turn left and ride up past old shack.
- **Mile 2.5**– turn right and then bear right at fork.
- **Mile 2.7**– turn sharply back uphill to the left.
- **Mile 3.4**– turn right, then bear right at fork.
- **Mile 3.8**– turn left up steep hill away from powerlines.
- **Mile 4.2**– turn right across creek and then bear right.
- **Mile 4.7**– turn right onto ridge.
- **Mile 5.8**– cross Volksmarch Trail.
- **Mile 6.4**– turn right into town to finish.

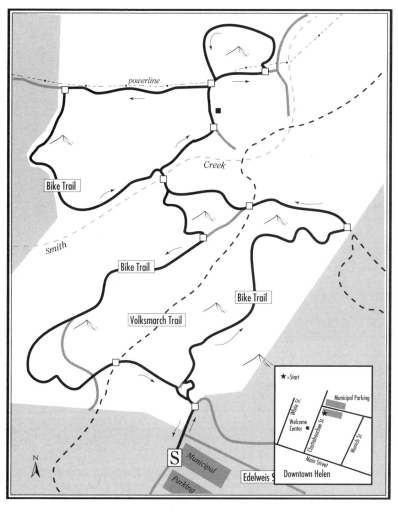

MAP KEY

Bike Route..........................	~
Other Trail or Road...........	~
Direction of Travel.................	→
Start/Finish.............................	S
Milepost..................................	□
Public Land......................	
Other Land.......................	
Recreation/Camping Area...	Δ
Major Mountain...................	
River, Lake or Stream.....	

Forest Service Rd. #.................	476
Road or Trail Name.....	Black Mountain Trail
Foot Travel Only.......	- - - -
Timber Cut or Clearing..	////

Elevation Change

1840'
1650'
1440'
1500'

MOST DIFFICULT TRAILS

26

North Pocket

Don't be dismayed with the first bit of trail, which is steep and washed out. Soon you'll find great curving single track that skirts an array of neat abandoned tunnels. The climb up to the top of the Pocket is rocky, demanding and sometimes impossible, while the return to the bottom is a challenge in itself.

Start/Finish

Take GA 193 west of LaFayette 8 miles to Davis Crossroads and turn left onto Hogjowl Road. Go 2.7 miles and turn left onto Pocket Road. It's 1.3 more miles to the trailhead.

Trail Configuration

Loop

Surface

Single track • 9.3 miles
Forest road • 1.6 miles

Highlights

Tunnels, views, stream crossings, severe washouts, horse use, very rocky climb, big waterfall

Total Distance

10.9 miles

Time Allowance

Beginner • not recommended
Intermediate • 4.5 hours
Advanced • 3 hours

Mileposts

- **From start**– ride out back of trailhead parking across creek onto **orange blazed** Mine Trail. Within the first mile you should start to see tunnel entrances.
- **Mile 2.4**– trail exits right. Stay on Mine Trail.
- **Mile 2.5**– cross creek and turn right onto forest road.
- **Mile 3.6**– bear right and start following **white blazes** of Cane Trail up the road.
- **Mile 4.1**– road ends. Trail begins. This is the beginning of the tough rocky, climbing section.
- **Mile 5**– a trail exits to the right. Stay on Cane Trail.
- **Mile 7.3**– end of difficult climb. Turn right and then right again onto **blue blazed** North Pocket Trail.
- **Mile 10.2**– continue onto forest road and past gate.
- **Mile 10.9**– finish.

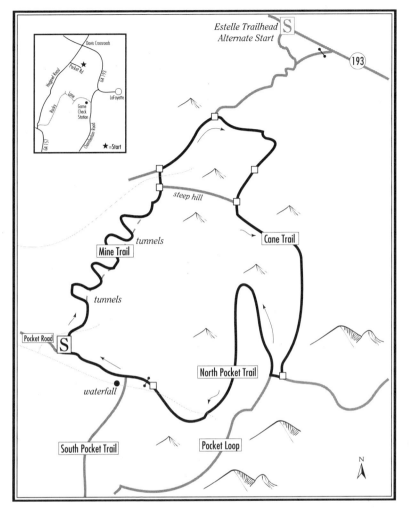

Estelle Trailhead
Alternate Start S

Daves Crossroads

Pocket Rd ★

Hogpen Road

GA 193

Rocky Lane

Game Check Station

Lafayette

GA 157

Chamberlain Road

★ =Start

193

steep hill

tunnels

Mine Trail

Cane Trail

tunnels

Pocket Road S

North Pocket Trail

waterfall

South Pocket Trail

Pocket Loop

N

MAP KEY

Bike Route............................ 〰

Other Trail or Road........... 〰

Direction of Travel................ ⟶

Start/Finish............................ S

Milepost.................................. □

Public Land........................ ▭

Other Land........................ ▭

Recreation/Camping Area... ⛺

Major Mountain.................... ⛰

River, Lake or Stream..... 〜

Forest Service Rd. #................. 476

Road or Trail Name..... Black Mountain Trail

Foot Travel Only....... ⌁

Timber Cut or Clearing.. ▨

920'   2110'

Elevation Change

27

Windy Gap

First, you'll take to the side of Grassy Mountain on the technical Milma Trail before making the long steep climb up Tibbs Trail to the highest point near Lake Conasauga. Hold onto your socks! The descent is steep, rocky, difficult and a real blast.

Start/Finish

From the stoplight in Eton, go east on CCC Camp Road 4.3 miles. Turn left on FS 218. It's 2 miles to the trailhead.

Trail Configuration

Loop with extension

Surface

Single track • 8.7 miles
Forest road • 2.2 miles

Highlights

Views, ORV and ATV use, steep climb, very technical downhill, banked turns

Total Distance

10.9 miles

Time Allowance

Beginner • 4 hours
Intermediate • 3 hours
Advanced • 2 hours

Mileposts

- **From start**– ride up Windy Gap Cycle Trail.
- **Mile 1.3**– begin loop by turning right onto Milma ATV Trail.
- **Mile 5.1**– turn left up Tibbs ORV Trail.
- **Mile 5.7**– continue past gate.
- **Mile 6.5**– turn left onto FS 68.
- **Mile 6.6**– bear left at fork. The right fork goes to Lake Conasauga Recreation Area.
- **Mile 7.3**– turn left down Windy Gap Cycle Trail.
- **Mile 9.6**– Milma Trail enters from left. Continue straight on Windy Gap Cycle Trail back to trailhead
- **Mile 10.9**– finish.

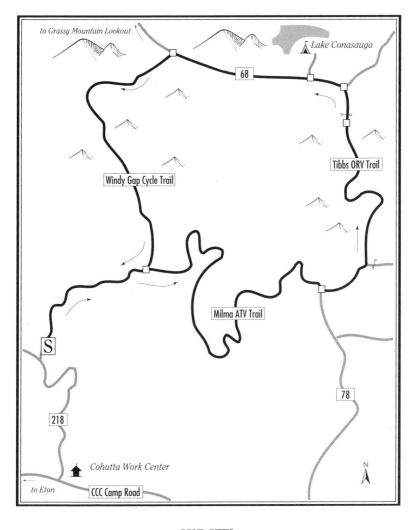

to Grassy Mountain Lookout

⛺ Lake Conasauga

68

Tibbs ORV Trail

Windy Gap Cycle Trail

S

Milma ATV Trail

78

218

Cohutta Work Center

to Eton

CCC Camp Road

N

MAP KEY

Bike Route............................ 〰	Forest Service Rd. #................. 476
Other Trail or Road........... 〰	Road or Trail Name..... Black Mountain Trail
Direction of Travel................ →	Foot Travel Only........ ‑ ‑ ‑ ‑ ‑
Start/Finish.............................. S	Timber Cut or Clearing.. ▨
Milepost.................................. □	
Public Land...................... ▭	
Other Land....................... ▬	
Recreation/Camping Area... ⛺	
Major Mountain................... 〰	
River, Lake or Stream..... 〰	

3263'

1260'

Elevation Change

28

Mountaintown Creek

This is one of the most remote rides in North Georgia. You'll climb to the ridge line bordering the Cohutta Wilderness before dropping down into the Mountaintown Creek Gorge with its many cascades and waterfalls. It's then a short ride through the valley before the long climb back to the trailhead.

Start/Finish

From milepost 8 on GA 52 west of Ellijay, take County Road #65 north for 5.4 miles. Continue onto FS 90 for another 1.7 miles, turn right onto FS 68 and go 2 miles to the trailhead parking area.

Trail Configuration

Loop

Surface

Single track • 5.4 miles
Forest road • 13.6 miles
Pavement • 0.6 miles

Highlights

Remote, views, cascades and waterfalls, multiple stream crossings, boggy areas, long climb, mountain farms

Total Distance

19.6 miles

Time Allowance

Beginner • 5 hours
Intermediate • 3.25 hours
Advanced • 2.5 hours

Mileposts

- **From start–** ride uphill on FS 68.
- **Mile 1.3–** turn right onto FS 64.
- **Mile 8–** turn right onto Mountaintown Creek Trail.
- **Mile 13.4–** lower trailhead for Mountaintown Creek Trail.
- **Mile 14–** pass pond on right. A road enters on the right and a little farther on a road enters on the left. Stay straight.
- **Mile 15.4–** turn right onto paved County Road #65.
- **Mile 15.8–** for an alternate return via the Bear Creek Trail, turn right here on FS 241. Otherwise, go straight.
- **Mile 16–** turn right onto gravel road which is FS 90.
- **Mile 17.6–** turn right onto FS 68.
- **Mile 19.6–** finish.

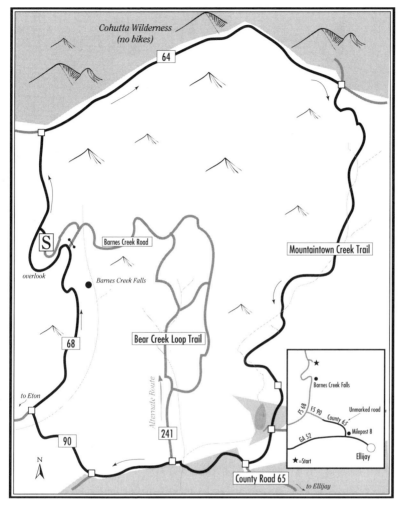

MAP KEY

Bike Route

Other Trail or Road

Direction of Travel

Start/Finish .... S

Milepost .... □

Public Land

Other Land

Recreation/Camping Area ... ⛺

Major Mountain

River, Lake or Stream

Forest Service Rd. # 476

Road or Trail Name ..... Black Mountain Trail

Foot Travel Only

Timber Cut or Clearing

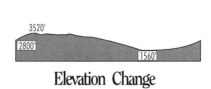

Elevation Change

3520'
2800'
1560'

MOST DIFFICULT TRAILS

29

Amicalola Falls

Starting with a top-of-Georgia view, you'll do a little climbing, then a hidden ATV trail takes you into a beautiful valley. You're not there long before making an arduous climb over Frosty Mountain and back to the falls.

Start/Finish
Amicalola Falls State Park.
Top of falls bike parking lot.

Trail Configuration
Loop w/ extension

Surface
Single/double track • 6.2 miles
Forest road • 9.6 miles

Highlights
Waterfall view, stream crossings, ATV use, very rocky sections

Total Distance
15.8 miles

Time Allowance
Beginner • 4.5 hours
Intermediate • 3 hours
Advanced • 2 hours

Mileposts
- **From start**– ride up bike trail from parking lot.
- **Mile 0.4**– turn right onto High Shoals Road.
- **Mile 1.6**– bear left at road fork to begin loop.
- **Mile 2.8**– ford two streams and then turn right onto ATV trail. It may not be marked with a sign.
- **Mile 4.9**– turn right onto FS 357.
- **Mile 6.8**– make 180° turn right onto FS 28.
- **Mile 7.1**– drive exits left. Bear right on FS 28.
- **Mile 7.3**– road forks. Bear right toward houses on FS 28.
- **Mile 9.6**– FS 6652 exits left. Stay on FS 28.
- **Mile 10.8**– Nimblewill Gap. Make 180° right turn onto jeep road and continue to climb. Do not go downhill. **Do not ride on Appalachian Trail Lead.**
- **Mile 11.9**– road forks. Bear left.
- **Mile 14.2**– turn left onto High Shoals Road.
- **Mile 15.4**– turn left onto bike trail.
- **Mile 15.8**– finish.

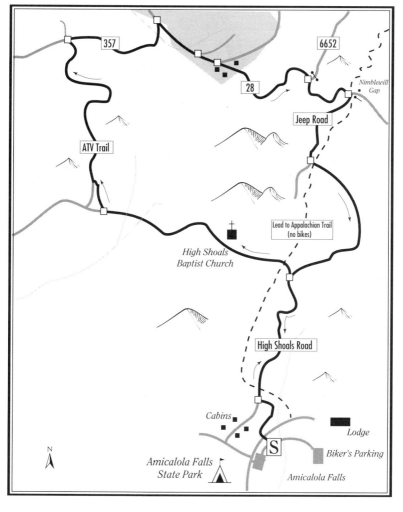

357

6652

28

Nimblewill
Gap

Jeep Road

ATV Trail

Lead to Appalachian Trail
(no bikes)

High Shoals
Baptist Church

High Shoals Road

Cabins

Lodge

S

Biker's Parking

Amicalola Falls
State Park

Amicalola Falls

N

MAP KEY

Bike Route............................	Forest Service Rd. #.................	476
Other Trail or Road...........	Road or Trail Name.....	Black Mountain Trail
Direction of Travel................ ⟶	Foot Travel Only.......	- - -
Start/Finish............................ S	Timber Cut or Clearing..	/////
Milepost..................................... □		
Public Land......................		
Other Land......................		
Recreation/Camping Area... ⛺		
Major Mountain..................		
River, Lake or Stream.....		

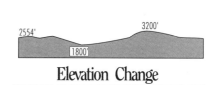

2554'   3200'

1800'

Elevation Change

30

Bull Mountain

A three-mile almost continuous climb, lots of single track, numerous small stream crossings, the sounds of waterfalls, miles of tight twisting downhill through the trees, rocky ascents and beautiful scenery—this route has it all! It's easy to see why it's so popular.

Start/Finish

From Nimblewill Baptist Church off GA 52 near Dahlonega, go 0.4 miles on FS 28 and turn left up FS 83. It's 1.8 miles to the trailhead. *Several biker parking lots are planned in the area. Until they are finished, find a convenient pulloff. Please don't use the horse parking area.*

Trail Configuration

Loop

Surface

Single track • 8.8 miles
Forest road • 2.1 miles

Highlights

Long hill climb, stream crossings, rhododendron tunnels, rocky sections, horse use, winter views

Total Distance

10.9 miles

Time Allowance

Beginner • 3+ hours
Intermediate • 2.5 hours
Advanced • 1.75 hours

Mileposts

- **From start**– ride up steps onto Bull Mountain Trail. It's marked with **orange diamond blazes**.
- **Mile 1.3**– whoop-te-do trail enters from right.
- **Mile 4.5**– old trail enters up from the right. Bear left to begin Bull Mountain Extension (aka: Bare Hare Trail).
- **Mile 8.5**– pass gate and turn left onto FS 77A.
- **Mile 8.7**– pass gate, turn right across creek and continue straight up the hill on the rocky roadbed.
- **Mile 9**– whoop-te-do trail exits right just before shack. Continue past shack, following the property line road between Forest Service and private land. Stay on the road. After passing the third shack on the left, the road leaves the property line and becomes a trail.
- **Mile 9.6**– turn right onto FS 83.
- **Mile 10.9**– finish.

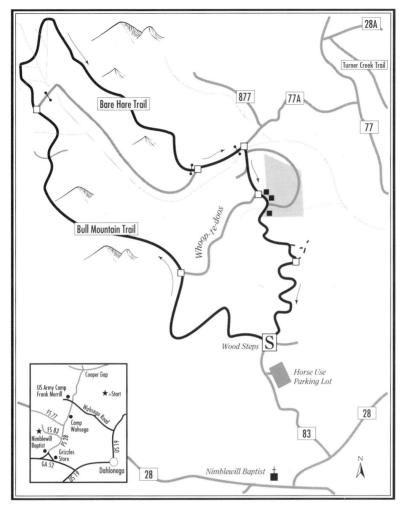

28A

Turner Creek Trail

Bare Hare Trail

877

77A

77

Bull Mountain Trail

Whoop-te-doos

Wood Steps   S

Horse Use
Parking Lot

28

Cooper Gap

US Army Camp
Frank Merrill   ★ =Start

Wahsega Road

FS 77

FS 83   Camp
★   Wahsega

Nimblewill
Baptist

Grizzles
Store

GA 52

US 19

Dahlonega

US 19

28

83

Nimblewill Baptist †

N

MAP KEY

Bike Route..........................	Forest Service Rd. #................. 476
Other Trail or Road..........	Road or Trail Name..... Black Mountain Trail
Direction of Travel...............	Foot Travel Only........
Start/Finish............................. S	Timber Cut or Clearing..
Milepost................................... □	
Public Land......................	
Other Land......................	
Recreation/Camping Area...	
Major Mountain..................	
River, Lake or Stream.....	

2510'

1760'

1787'

Elevation Change

31

Tennessee Divide

A long, steep climb takes you up to the Tennessee Divide. All the water behind you goes to the Gulf via the Chattahoochee River. All the water ahead of you goes to the Gulf via the Tennessee River. You'll cross and recross the divide before making a speedy return back down to the Hooch.

Start/Finish

From Helen, drive 1 mile north on GA 17/75. Turn left on Alt. 75. Cross river and turn right on FS 44. Go 2.9 miles to Game Check Station. *If it's hunting season, find a convenient pulloff.*

Trail Configuration

Loop

Surface

Forest road • 19.1 miles
Pavement • 4.7 miles

Highlights

Great views, long strenuous climb, loose gravel, highway, river and stream crossings, waterfall

Total Distance

23.8 miles

Time Allowance

Beginner • 4 hours
Intermediate • 3 hours
Advanced • 2.25 hours

Mileposts

- **From start–** ride south, back down FS 44.
- **Mile 0.7–** start loop and continue on FS 44.
- **Mile 3.1–** turn left onto GA Alt. 75, then left on 17/75.
- **Mile 3.9–** turn right onto FS 79 and start 3-mile climb.
- **Mile 9.8–** road forks. Bear left downhill onto FS 283.
- **Mile 10.4–** Indian Grave Gap. Continue on FS 283.
  Do not ride on Appalachian Trail.
- **Mile 12.6–** side hike to High Shoals Falls.
- **Mile 13.9–** turn left onto GA 17/75. Start 2-mile climb.
- **Mile 15.9–** Unicoi Gap. Just past gap, turn right on FS 44.
- **Mile 17.9–** turn left onto FS 178 and go around gate.
- **Mile 23.1–** turn right onto FS 44.
- **Mile 23.8–** finish.

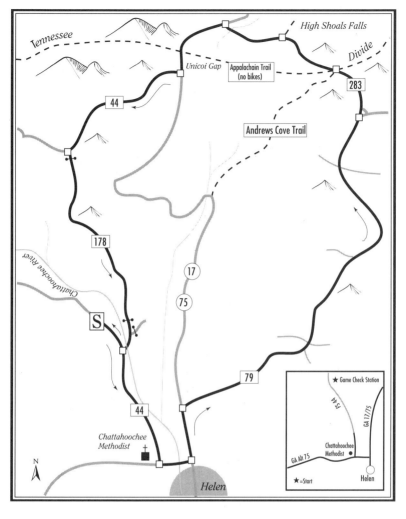

High Shoals Falls

Tennessee

Divide

Unicoi Gap

Appalachain Trail
(no bikes)

283

44

Andrews Cove Trail

178

17

75

79

Chattahoochee River

S

44

Chattahoochee
Methodist

N

Helen

★ Game Check Station

FS 44

GA 17/75

GA Alt 75

Chattahoochee
Methodist

★ =Start

Helen

MAP KEY

Bike Route........................... 〜

Other Trail or Road........... 〜

Direction of Travel................ ⟶

Start/Finish............................. Ⓢ

Milepost.................................. ▫

Public Land.....................

Other Land.....................

Recreation/Camping Area... ⛺

Major Mountain...................

River, Lake or Stream.....

Forest Service Rd. #................. 476

Road or Trail Name..... Black Mountain Trail

Foot Travel Only....... ⟋ ⎯ ⎯ ⎯

Timber Cut or Clearing.. ⫽⫽⫽

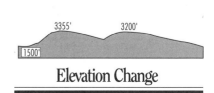

3355'   3200'

1500'

Elevation Change

Regional Information

Local Bike Resources
Lodging & Camping
Weather Chart
SORBA

Local Bike Resources

Bike Shops

- **Dalton Bicycle Works**
  1107 E. Walnut Ave.
  Dalton, GA 30721
  706/279-2558
  *Close to Cohuttas and
  Pigeon Mountain*

- **Recycled Cycles**
  Rt. 5, Box 244
  Ellijay, GA 30540
  706/635-BIKE
  *Close to Cohuttas,
  Carters Lake, Aska Trails,
  Amicalola Falls, and Bull
  Mountain Trails*

- **East Ridge Bicycles**
  5910 Ringold Road
  Chattanooga, TN 37412
  423/894-9122
  Close to Pigeon Mountain

- **Mountain Adventures Cyclery**
  Hwy 400 and Hwy 60
  Long Branch Station #11
  Dahlonega, GA 30533
  706/864-8525
  *Close to Amicalola Falls, Bull
  Mountain Area and Helen*

- **Bike Town USA**
  1604 Dawsonville Hwy.
  Gainesville, GA 30501
  706/532-7090
  *Close to Amicalola Falls, Bull
  Mountain Area and Helen*

- **Tallulah Point Overlook**
  Tallulah Gorge Scenic Loop
  Tallulah Falls, GA 30573
  706/754-4318
  *Close to Tallulah Gorge
  and Helen*

Lodging & Camping

Camping in the Chattahoochee National Forest

There are a good number of Forest Service recreation areas located within the Chattahoochee National Forest. Each has campsites with picnic tables and many have drinking water and restroom facilities. These are open from late May through early September and sites may be taken on a first-come, first-served basis. A small fee is charged.

If roughing it is more your style, you may camp anywhere in the national forest that is not posted "no camping." No charge or permit is required. There are many primitive campsites along the forest roads, as well.

Georgia State Parks

Georgia has an excellent system of state parks that not only feature recreational opportunities, but offer a wide range of overnight accommodations as well. Each park found in the North Georgia area has primitive camping, full-hookup camping, and rental cottages. Of those, several have lodges, conference centers, and restaurants. It's wise to call ahead for reservations, especially for the summer or fall leaf seasons.

- **Unicoi State Park & Lodge**
  P.O. Box 1029
  Helen, GA 30545
  706/878-2824 or 706/878-3366

- **Vogel State Park**
  Route 1, Box 1230
  Blairsville, GA 30512
  706/745-2628

- **Amicalola Falls State Park & Lodge**
  Star Route, Box 215
  Dawsonville, GA 30534
  706/265-8888

- **Tallulah Gorge State Park**
  P.O. Box 248
  Tallulah Falls, GA 30573
  706/754-8257

Local Chambers of Commerce

In addition to the camping areas on public lands and state park lodges, North Georgia has a wide assortment of hotels, motels, lodges and bed & breakfasts. If you are looking for this type of accommodation, it's best to call ahead to the town or towns nearest your biking destination and check with the local chamber of commerce (number listed below) for up-to-date information.

- **LaFayette**
  706/375-7702

- **Chatsworth**
  706/695-6060

- **Ellijay**
  706/635-7400

- **Blue Ridge**
  706/632-5680

- **Dahlonega**
  706/864-3513

- **Helen**
  706/878-2521

- **Clarksville**
  706/754-3097

- **Clayton**
  706/782-4812

Weather Chart

Month	Average Temperature*	Average Rainfall (in inches)
January	41°	5.5"
February	43°	4"
March	50°	7"
April	60°	4.9"
May	67°	5.7"
June	75°	4.7"
July	78°	5"
August	76°	4"
September	71°	4"
October	60°	2.5"
November	50°	3.5"
December	43°	4"

*All temperatures are Fahrenheit. Information provided by the National Weather Service.

SORBA
Southern Off-Road Bicycle Association

SORBA is a volunteer nonprofit organization formed to promote trail preservation and development, mountain bike racing, touring, and fun and fellowship for all mountain bicyclists in the Southeast. The *Fat Tire Times, Land Access Alert* and special flyers are published as a means of keeping members informed of current issues, rides, work parties, races and other events. Annually, the SORBA Fat Tire Festival is held to raise funds for land access and trail maintenance projects and to just have fun. Membership in SORBA entitles you to a year's subscription to *Fat Tire Times, Land Access Alert*, special mailings—and a whole lot of fun!

MEMBERSHIP APPLICATION

SORBA
P.O. Box 671774
Marietta, GA 30067

NAME: _____
          (Last)   (First)   (Initial)

ADDRESS: _____

CITY _____ STATE _____ ZIP _____ PHONE (H) _____

                                           (W) _____

AGE: _____

OTHER CLUB AFFILIATIONS: _____

TYPE OF MEMBERSHIP: Individual ($10) _____   Renewal _____

                               Family ($15) _____   Changes _____

                               Organization ($20)_____   Land Access Fund _____

In consideration of my membership, I agree not to hold the Southern Off-Road Bicycle Association, Inc., or any of its members, liable for any injury or damage, however caused, which may result from participation in any event sponsored by SORBA.

Signature: _____
Parents or Guardian if under 18: _____

Notes

Notes

Notes